Leading
with
Soul

Lee G. Bolman

Terrence E. Deal

Leading
with
Soul

An Uncommon Journey of Spirit

New and Revised Edition

JOSSEY-BASS
A Wiley Company
San Francisco

Published by

JOSSEY-BASS
A Wiley Company
350 Sansome St.
San Francisco, CA 94104

www.josseybass.com

Jossey-Bass books and products are available through most bookstores. To contact
Jossey-Bass directly, call (888) 378-2537, fax to (800) 605-2665, or visit our
website at www.josseybass.com.

Substantial discounts on bulk quantities of Jossey-Bass books are available to
corporations, professional associations, and other organizations. For details and
discount information, contact the special sales department at Jossey-Bass.

Interior design by Nancy Sayre Simerly
Illustrations by Barbara Rhodes
Credits are on page 259.

We at Jossey-Bass strive to use the most environmentally sensitive paper stocks available
to us. Our publications are printed on acid-free recycled stock whenever possible, and
our paper always meets or exceeds minimum GPO and EPA requirements.

Library of Congress Cataloging-in-Publication Data

Bolman, Lee G.
  Leading with soul : an uncommon journey of spirit / Lee G. Bolman,
Terrence E. Deal.— New and rev. ed.
    p. cm.
Includes bibliographical references.
  ISBN 0-7879-5547-7 (alk. paper)
  1. Leadership—Moral and ethical aspects. 2.
Leadership—Religious aspects. I. Deal, Terrence E. II. Title.
  HD57.7 .B64 2001
  658.4'092—dc21   2001000322

SECOND EDITION
HB Printing   10 9 8 7 6 5 4 3 2 1

For

Barry Edwin Deal   August 17, 1959–November 28, 1964

Eldred Ross Bolman   March 3, 1914–May 4, 1985

Florence Bernice Bolman   August 26, 1915–June 28, 1999

CONTENTS

Prelude
In Search of Soul and Spirit   3

The Search
1. The Heart of Leadership Lives in the Hearts of Leaders   17
2. The Human Heart Is More Than a Pump   25
3. The Journey of a Soul   29
4. Discovering New Teachers   33

INTERLUDE: Reclaiming Your Soul   39

Conviction
5. A Place to Start   51
6. Vicissitudes of the Journey   55

INTERLUDE: Leaning into Your Fear   61

Gifts
7. Gifts of Leadership   71
8. Authorship   77

CONTENTS

9. Love   83

10. Power   91

11. Significance   97

INTERLUDE: Community and the Cycle of Giving   105

Sharing
12. Summoning the Magic of Stories   123

13. Lifting Our Voices in Song   131

14. Celebrating Shared Icons   139

INTERLUDE: Expressing the Spirit   145

A New Life
15. The Twilight of Leadership   155

16. Deep Refuge   163

INTERLUDE: The Cycle of the Spirit   167

17. The Legacy   179

Postlude
Continuing a Spirited Dialogue   185

Soul at Work   213

CONTENTS

Notes   237
Recommended Reading   245
Acknowledgments   249
The Authors   255
Write to the Authors   257

Leading
with
Soul

❦

Prelude

In Search of Soul and Spirit

All day I think about it, then at night I say it.
Where did I come from,
   and what am I supposed to be doing?
I have no idea.
My soul is from elsewhere, I'm sure of that,
and I intend to end up there.

                              —*Rumi*

Soul. The word sometimes sounds strange to the modern ear. Terms like *heart* and *spirit* seem almost as exotic. We rarely think or talk about where we came from or what we are here to do. We need to. Otherwise, we deaden our souls, stunt our spirits, and live our lives halfheartedly.

The search for soul and spirit, for depth and meaning in our lives, is fueling a powerful and growing twenty-first-century movement. It is a contemporary quest for depth, meaning, and faith that transcends boundaries of gender, age, geography, and race. It's as fresh and contemporary and specific to our time as the latest dot-com start-up. It's emerging as a counterforce to the modern technical mind-set that can land a man on the moon yet provides few answers for bringing joy to life or meaning to work.

At the same time this contemporary search is grounded in the age-old journey of the soul that has been a core preoccupation of every human culture since the beginning of time. Over the centuries, people have found meaning in work, family, community, and shared faith. They have drawn upon collective resources to do what they could not do alone. United efforts—raising a barn, shoring a levee, rescuing earthquake victims, celebrating a marriage, or singing a hymn—have brought people together, created enduring bonds, and exemplified the possibilities in collective spirit. Such traditional sources of meaning, energy, and achievement are now seriously endangered. More and more individuals are pondering a question posed by Jesus two thousand years ago: What does it profit us if we gain the world but lose our souls?[1]

The signs of spiritual hunger and restlessness are everywhere. Something's missing—an elusive, nagging something. Not long ago, Warren Bennis asked a group of young dot-com millionaires about their work and reported: "They were vaguely disconsolate—despairing—something 'beyond words' one told me, 'something missing.' A severe case of affluenza, I thought. I also wondered: 'What was missing?'"[2]

We are convinced that what's really missing is soul and spirit. Some people experience this gap as a haunting sense that somewhere along the line they got off track. They're working harder than ever, but they're not sure why, and they've lost touch with what's really important in life. For others, life feels like a forced march. They can never get off the treadmill, even though they don't know where they're going. Still others feel it as a vague emptiness that pursues them relentlessly as they rush madly through life. They hope they can escape if they keep running. Deep down, they know they're losing the race. There are count-less other ways individuals may experience this sense of spiritual emptiness: as a lack of zest and joy, as ennui, as depression, as an aching, debilitating impression that one's life is going nowhere.

All these experiences are clues, symptoms of spiritual malaise—a hollow, existential vacuum that can be filled only by a greater attention to soul, spirit, and faith. This disease of the spirit often feels unique and personal. And it is. But it's also shared. Too many workplaces are almost devoid of meaning and purpose. They are ruled by technology, efficiency, and the bottom line, with little regard for what human beings need in order to experience personal fulfillment and success. Over time, this takes a heavy toll on motivation, loyalty, and performance. It is a road to crisis and decay—unless we find ways to reinfuse the workplace with passion, zest, and spirit.

More and more people are working to recapture the essence of what soul and spirit can bring to the modern workplace. As Matthew Fox writes: "Life and livelihood ought not to be separated but to flow from the same source, which is Spirit, for both life and livelihood are about Spirit. Spirit means life, and both life and livelihood are about living in depth, living with meaning, purpose, joy, and a sense of contribution to the greater community. A spirituality of work is about bringing life and livelihood back together again. And spirit with them."[3]

The reemergence of spirituality has grown well beyond the yearnings of a few lost souls. It's evolving into a broad social movement, a shared undertaking. It needs to be shared, because we can't all go it alone. This movement is gathering strength not just in North America but throughout the world. Just one indicator of this growth is that the first edition of *Leading with Soul* has been translated for readers in Asia, Europe, Latin America, and the Middle East. Letters to the authors from readers around the world sound remarkably similar themes and raise many of the same questions. In the Postlude we share some of those questions and our responses to them. We also invite readers to continue the dialogue.

Even before the first edition of this book came out, we had begun to share its message with a variety of audiences. The depth and power of their responses were surprising and gratifying. People thanked us for saying things that needed to be said, for putting words to concerns they had struggled to voice, and for validating a dialogue that they were eager to have with colleagues, friends, and family.

When we began hearing from readers who accepted our first edition invitation to write and share personal reactions, the calls and letters brought moving stories of individual readers' own journeys—sometimes heartwarming, sometimes poignant. We heard from scores of individuals who were searching for a more meaningful life at work and at home. Of course, not all reactions to *Leading with Soul* have been positive. Our friend Father Paul

Keenan, himself an author and the host of a New York City talk show, read reviews of our book and concluded that there was little middle ground. The book, in his view, hits people in one of two ways: either they like it a lot or they think it's worthless.[4]

Over time, both readers and critics have helped us understand why reactions have been so polarized. As one perceptive reviewer noted, the book requires readers to step out of customary modes of reading passively in search of answers or information. It asks them instead to become active and engaged by reflecting on and interpreting the text's meaning for them. What readers bring to the text and find between the lines is even more important than what we have written. This book works to the degree that people become active coauthors and cocreators. Many readers have done this so well that they have found messages that go well beyond anything we can take credit for. We have also heard from readers who found little in the book on first reading yet reported that it had a powerful, even dramatic impact when they revisited it a year or two later.

When *Leading with Soul* first appeared, it was part of a tiny trickle of books addressing spirituality at work. The trickle has since grown into a tide that shows no signs of ebbing.[5] In that outpouring is a rich and yeasty diversity of voices and approaches. Some books approach spirituality in the context of a specific religious tradition, such as Christianity, Judaism, or Buddhism. Some focus on a specific practice, such as meditation. Some are handbooks or primers offering suggestions and guidelines for adding spiritual depth to one's life. But almost all focus on soul and spirit.

Soul and spirit are so interconnected that the two words are often used interchangeably, but we see an important distinction. Soul is personal and unique, grounded in the depths of personal experience. When each of us plunges into the depths at the core of our being, there we find soul. Spirit is transcendent and all embracing. It is the universal source, the oneness of all things: God, Jahweh, Allah, and the Buddha. Soul and spirit are related in the same way as peaks and valleys, male and female. They are intimately connected. Each needs the other. Leaders with soul bring spirit to organizations. They marry the two so that spirit feeds soul rather than starving it and soul enriches spirit rather than killing it. Leaders of spirit find their soul's treasure store and offer its gifts to others.[6]

Books about spirituality often speak from a specific religious tradition. That is not our objective. It has been said that "spirituality is the goal, religion is the path."[7] But it is not the only path. The word *religion* implies a group of people bound together by a vision of the divine expressed through shared beliefs, institutions, rituals, and artifacts. Every great religion offers special gifts based on its unique spiritual tradition. Other paths fall outside established religion. Alcoholics Anonymous offers its widely respected, highly successful twelve-step program to help its members find meaning in a life without alcohol. AA's approach is explicitly spiritual, insisting that members place their trust not in themselves but in a higher power. At the same time, individuals are free to interpret that power as they choose.

Leading with Soul has an ecumenical intent. Ours is a diverse and inclusive caravan, and we invite spiritual seekers of all backgrounds and persuasions to join us in the search for something bigger. Our goal is not to teach a specific theology or philosophy but to pose questions and stimulate reflection to help you deepen the faith you have or find the one you need. We invite you to become a coauthor. Treat the stories and ideas in these pages as a stimulus and a starting point. Test them against your own knowledge and experience. Talk to yourself and your friends, and talk back to us. Ask hard questions. Fill in the gaps and holes you find in what we have produced by writing your own story and exploring your own path. Look for opportunities to share your reflections and questions with others. Talk about the path you and your family or you and your colleagues are following. Where is your journey taking you? Is that really where you want to go?

As someone once observed, follow the highway and you'll probably arrive at a destination; follow your heart and you may leave a trail.

We particularly hope that this book will stimulate a journey in search of your leadership gifts. Each of us has a special contribution to make if we can shoulder the personal and spiritual work needed to discover and take responsibility for our own gifts. Across sectors and levels, organizations are starved for the leadership they need. Two misleading images currently dominate organizational thinking about leadership: one the heroic champion with extraordinary stature and vision, the other the "policy wonk," the skilled analyst who solves pressing problems with information, programs, and policies. Both these images emphasize the hands and heads of leaders, neglecting deeper and more enduring elements of courage, spirit, and hope. Leaders who have lost touch with their own souls, who are confused and uncertain about their core values and beliefs, inevitably lose their way or sound an uncertain trumpet.

It is easy to go astray when we forget that the heart of leadership is in the hearts of leaders. We fool ourselves, thinking that sheer bravado or analytical techniques can respond to our deepest concerns. We lose touch with the deepest and most precious of human gifts—soul and spirit. To recapture spirit, we need to relearn how to lead with soul: How to know ourselves and our faith at the deepest level. How to breathe new zest and buoyancy into life. How to reinvigorate the family as a sanctuary where people can grow, develop, and find love. How to reinfuse the workplace with vigor and élan. Leading with soul returns us to ancient spiritual basics—reclaiming the enduring human capacity that gives our lives passion and purpose.

The chapters ahead explore soul, spirit, and faith and why they belong at the heart of leadership. They do this through a dialogue between a beleaguered leader and a wise sage. Over the centuries, spiritual leaders of all traditions and faiths have taught and learned through example, story, and dialogue. Christian and Sufi parables, Zen koans, the Jewish Haggadah, Hindu legends, and Native American stories are but a few examples. In our story, you are invited to join Steve Camden, a highly successful, fast-track manager who has run into an existential wall, as he works with Maria, a spiritual mentor. Many readers, both men and women, have told us they identify with Steve—his confusion, his yearning, his sense of being lost and stuck. Many have also told us they were fortunate enough to have a Maria who provided them critical guidance at key moments in their lives. Others have written to say they desperately need a Maria and wonder if we know where to find one.

This story is a parable drawn from the authors' own lives and the lives of others we have known. We hope it speaks to you. To assist your reflections, we punctuate the story with a series of interludes—meditations on the issues and questions raised in the story. Some readers tell us the interludes were indispensable in clarifying and deepening their reading experience. Others report the opposite—the interludes were unwelcome interruptions, and they preferred to follow the story straight through. As a co-adventurer, you should choose the path through the book that works best for you. We also commend to you the counsel of Walt Whitman:

> Sail forth—steer for the deep waters only,
> Reckless O soul, exploring, I with thee,
>   and thou with me,
> For we are bound where mariner has not yet
>   dared to go,
> And we will risk the ship, ourselves and all.
> O my brave soul!
> O farther farther sail!
> O daring joy, but safe! are they not all the
>   seas of God?[8]

The Search

CHAPTER 1

The Heart of Leadership Lives in the Hearts of Leaders

His name was Steven Camden. Like the city in New Jersey. He grew up in New Jersey, but in Newark, not Camden. Not that it made much difference. There were tough neighborhoods in both places. He had learned to survive in one of the toughest.

He was tired, and it was getting dark. He had just driven three hours up this mountain from the city. Why? He still wasn't sure. Why had John sent him? He climbed the fieldstone steps and knocked on her door. He waited. Was she here? She knew he was coming, didn't she? She must know that he had better things to do than just stand on her doorstep. He looked again and she was there.

Her name was Maria. He first noticed her eyes: deep, brown, full of something he recognized but could not name. Once inside, he looked around the room. Mostly he noticed the Japanese art.

It was like a gallery. But something was missing. What?

You've spent time in Japan, he said.

She nodded. Many years. Every piece is a memory.

I lived in Tokyo two years myself.

For him, Tokyo had been an endless series of business meetings. No time for galleries. All his souvenirs came from the duty-free shop in the Tokyo airport.

She seemed to be waiting. Was he supposed to make the next

move? Where to begin? Blurt out his worries to a woman he barely knew? He tried to buy time.

John seems to have a lot of confidence in you, he said.

We're old friends. I knew him back when he was starting your organization. We've become even closer since he retired. I've learned a lot from him.

Now what? She seemed to be waiting again. He'd always been good with words. Where were they now?

Do you feel uncomfortable here? she asked.

No. He hesitated. Well, maybe a little. Maybe I shouldn't have come.

Have some tea. He watched her pour the tea. He wanted coffee, but took the tea.

You've been working hard?

All my life. He sipped his tea. Green tea. Reminded him of Japan. He'd ordered it many times. *Nihon cha, kudasai.* A comforting sense of nostalgia.

Why? she asked.

Why what? He'd lost track.

Why do you work so hard?

He'd never thought about it. He paused. Why does anyone work hard? It's what you do. It's how I got where I am.

Do you like where you are?

Of course. He was lying. He knew it. Did she? Probably.

Well, maybe not. Not as much as I used to.

What's changed?

He hesitated. Should he tell her the truth? What did he have to lose? He vaguely imagined John looking over his shoulder.

I was promoted a year ago. They put me in charge of one of our subsidiaries. I was sure I was ready.

And now?

He stared at the cranes delicately circling the outside of his teacup. Until this job, everything went right. Fast track. People seemed to think I could walk on water. Maybe it was talent, maybe luck, maybe just a lot of sweat. Whatever, it's not working any more.

You feel discouraged? She sounded sincere, maybe even caring. Why did she make him so nervous?

Like I'm on a treadmill. Running faster and faster. Getting farther and farther behind.

You need to get off.

I didn't need to drive three hours to learn that. I'm trying. He knew he sounded impatient. That's how he felt.

What have you tried?

Just about everything. Better time management. A mission

statement. Strategic planning. Reengineering. Training. A quality program.

Why was she staring at him? Why so silent? Did she think he'd done the wrong things? That he hadn't done enough?

He continued. I've sent executives to a management program. Top rating in *Business Week*. Hired consultants. World-class guys with world-class fees. I read *Fortune* and the *Harvard Business Review*. I talk to my boss.

She laughed. Why do you do all those things?

Her laughter grated. He felt his shoulders tighten. Was she laughing at him?

It worked in the past. Why not now?

She turned serious. What do you want from me?

The question stung. What did he really want? He groped for an answer. His mouth felt dry.

My work is my life. Always has been. What I always wanted. But a lot of the fun is gone. My boss is getting restless. It's the first time I ever felt I might fail in a job.

What's not working? she asked.

He told her about needing unity, but people's never agreeing. He said he needed a vision, but it was hard to see beyond next week. He told her he was lost. Things seemed to be falling apart. He'd never felt that way before.

She said she'd been there. That she understood.

Where had she been? Did she really understand? He wanted to say something. No words came.

And your spirit? she asked.

He looked to the door. He wanted to run. Get some fresh air. Get away from this crazy woman. Somehow, he couldn't move. Spirit? he stammered.

Yes, your spirit. Her tone was firm, assured. As if it were a perfectly normal question. Was she serious?

What do you mean?

Spirit. The internal force that sustains meaning and hope.

He was squirming. Was it a mistake for him to come?

A business is what you make it, she said calmly. If you believe it's a machine, it will be. A temple? It can be that too. Spirit and faith are the core of human life. Without them, you lose your way. You live without zest. You go through the motions, but there's no passion.

He was frustrated. He felt the anger building. He'd driven three hours for this? Teeth clenched, he told her what he felt. Look, I'm running an organization, not a church.

Her eyes fixed on his. She smiled. What do you hope to run it with? More sweat? More control? More tricks and gimmicks?

Maybe some wisdom. He hadn't meant to say that, but it came out anyway.

Wisdom will come. First, you have to look into your heart.

He was squirming again. Embarrassed. He could feel the blood rushing to his face. Why was he still here? Why didn't he get up and walk out?

You sound like my mother, he said scornfully. Follow your heart, she always said. She never really understood business.

Do you? she asked.

Of course.

Then, set a new course. You want to lead, don't you?

He nodded glumly. She continued.

The heart of leadership is in the hearts of leaders. You have to lead from something deep in your heart.

Like what?

I can't tell you what's in your heart, nor would you want me to. Would you want someone to offer you fruit but chew it up before giving it to you? No one can find meaning for you. Not your consultants, not your boss, not the *Harvard Business Review*. Only you really know what's in your heart.

He felt a twinge in his chest. A coincidence? He knew he'd been working too hard.

This isn't what you expected, she said.

Not at all.

It feels strange?

She was right. She seemed to know everything. Maybe a little, he admitted, wishing he hadn't.

She poured him more tea. You've been in uncomfortable situations before, haven't you?

Sure.

Have you learned from them?

He tried to review all his awkward moments. He gave up. There had been too many.

Usually.

Good. Then, shall we continue?

Continue what? A senseless conversation? Still, she seemed to be onto something. Something he couldn't quite grasp.

Maybe. I'm not sure.

Would you like some time to reflect?

A walk maybe.

Try the garden. Let's talk more when you get back.

CHAPTER 2

The Human Heart Is More Than a Pump

The walk helped. A chance to clear his head. He'd been told she was good. Very good. But she wasn't making sense. Off in the ozone. Talk more, she'd said. About what?

He found her reading in her study. Look, he said. Heart and spirit can wait. I've got problems *now!*

She looked up from her book. Perhaps that *is* your problem.

His jaw tightened. He was tired of playing games. He spat out, What the hell are you talking about?

About you. She paused, looking at him. You're decisive. You get things done.

Yeah. She's starting to get it, he thought.

You think things through. You're a good analyst.

True.

You take charge. You're on top of things.

One of my strengths. He was feeling better now. She was beginning to understand him.

Maybe your biggest weakness.

Was this a trap? He hated weakness. He felt his face flush again. He could barely control his rage.

Look, I'm a manager, not a social worker. You've got to be tough to get ahead.

How tough?

Why couldn't she get it? Put her in her place, then get out of here.

I'd heard you could help. Obviously bad advice. You're off the mark. Wasting my time. You're . . .

She laughed gently. At him?

I'm sorry, he said. I don't mean to offend you. Why was he apologizing? She should be the one to make amends.

Are you trying to scare me away? she asked.

26

She was right. She was getting too close. She'd triggered an old pattern. When you feel vulnerable, go on the attack.

OK, I'm upset. I'm tired. I'm looking for help.

Maybe your head and hands have taken you as far as they can.

Suppose that's true. Then what?

Try a new route. A journey of the heart.

A journey of the heart? Sounds like a TV soap opera.

Your heart is more than a pump. It's your spiritual center. It's courage and compassion. If you lose heart, life is empty, lonely. You're always busy but never fulfilled.

He felt panicky. He wanted to protest, but the words wouldn't come. Then it hit him. Right in the pit of his stomach. Maybe she's right.

You've had a long day, she said.

He nodded.

Get some rest. We'll talk more in the morning.

CHAPTER 3

The Journey of a Soul

The path curved gently up the mountainside. Above, a canopy of pine and spruce filtered the morning sun. Below, a blanket of wildflowers and a lake. Beautiful, he thought. The smells and sounds of spring surrounded them.

I love it here, she said.

I can see why. I should do this more often. He couldn't remember his last walk in the woods. Too little time. Too much to do.

If you let it, nature lifts your spirit. It touches your heart.

Spirit. Heart. Again. What was she talking about?

A journey of the heart, he said. How about a road map?

It's an inward journey. There's no map. You find your soul by looking deep within. There you discover your spiritual center.

I was hoping for something more concrete.

How can I give you directions to your soul?

Are you a therapist?

No.

Some kind of religious nut?

She laughed. Does the word soul scare you?

No, no. He was nervous. Puzzled. Not scared. There wasn't much that frightened him.

It's just that I didn't come here for sermons. I want answers.

Are you finding them?

No. That's why I'm here.

An old sage was once walking along a path very much like this one. Another man, not much younger than you, approached from the other direction. The young man's eyes were so riveted to the path that he bumped into the sage. The sage looked at the young man sternly and asked him where he was going. 'To catch my future,' the young man replied. 'How do you know you haven't already passed it?' the sage asked.

He hated to admit it, but he saw a resemblance. He was like the young man in the story.

You're talking about me?

Do you think so?

Eyes front. Tunnel vision.
He was conceding more
than he wanted.

She continued up the
path. She didn't seem
surprised. Same Mona Lisa
expression. Same warm, soft tone.

A journey of the soul is a quest
through uncharted territory. You find
your way by opening your eyes. And
your heart.

A ground squirrel scam-
pered across the path. It
seemed to know where it was going.
Why didn't he?

So where do I begin? he asked.

Where you are.

I'm not sure where that is.

That's a good beginning.

For what?

For your journey.

What if I'm not in a mood for traveling?

You won't be at first.

Why?

Because you're starting to realize that what you're looking for is directly ahead—on the very path you're afraid of taking.

They came to a stream and sat down. They sat in silence, watching a leaf float past.

CHAPTER 4

Discovering New Teachers

See that leaf. It wends its way to wherever the stream is taking it, she observed.

Look, I'm not a leaf. He meant to sound forceful. I'm a manager. My job is to control things, not be controlled.

She moved closer. Looked directly at him. Her eyes felt penetrating. Are you succeeding?

Maybe not. Not anymore.

Control is an illusion. It's seductive because it gives a feeling of power. Something to hold on to. So it becomes addictive. It's hard to give up even when it's not working. You can't start a journey until you let go of habits holding you back.

Tell it to my boss. I'm paid to be in charge.

That's the illusion. Look again at the water going by. There is a story about a stream that flowed around many obstacles until it arrived at a desert. The stream tried to cross, but its waters disappeared into the sand.

What's this got to do with me?

Maybe you and the stream have something in common.

Such as?

In the past, you always got past obstacles. Now you have a desert to cross.

That's a stretch. But if the stream found any answers, fill me in. I haven't heard any since I got here.

She seemed to ignore his sarcasm. The stream heard a voice. It said, 'The wind crosses the desert. So can the stream.' The stream protested, 'The wind can fly but I cannot.' The voice responded, 'Let yourself be absorbed by the wind.' The stream rebelled. 'I want to remain the same stream I am today.' 'Not possible,' said the voice. 'But your essence can be carried away and become a stream again. You've forgotten your essence.' The stream remembered dimly that she had once been held in the wind. She let her vapor rise into the arms of the wind, which carried it across the desert and then let it fall in the mountains. There it again became a stream.

Evaporation won't work for me.

Probably not. But letting go might.

Letting go of what?

The defenses you're using to push me away. The mind-set that's got you stuck.

He looked away. He stared at the stream for several minutes. Let go. Of what? Of something

he had clutched tightly for too long. He watched another leaf, trying to hold back the feelings welling up. They came anyway.

He spoke slowly, his voice cracking.

In the story, the stream remembered a time long before when the wind had held it. Being held in the past. He hesitated, waiting for a wave of feelings to pass. I was five when my father died. Sweetest guy in the world. Never stayed in a job. Left me and my mom with nothing. We didn't talk about him much. The message was always, 'Don't be like him. Make something of yourself.'

Have you followed that advice?

It worked. At least I thought so. Maybe I have lost something. Somewhere along the way.

You've lost touch with your soul.

If that's true, where do I look?

Inside. Outside. Your soul is inside, at your core. Teachers outside can help you find it.

Which teachers?

They're all around you.

Been to dozens of seminars. Workshops. Taught by top people. I didn't always learn that much.

Did any of them mention soul?

No. They usually don't. Not in management seminars.

She laughed. At least she had a sense of humor.

You're looking in the wrong places, she said. Life's deepest lessons are often where you least expect them. •

Like the school of hard knocks.

Sometimes the lessons are very hard. I remember a man who met regularly with a group of friends. One day, he said to his friends, 'I have discovered a new teacher. It's called AIDS.'

AIDS had hit his old neighborhood hard. This story cut deep. Beyond his usual defenses. He tried to dam the emotion coming from somewhere deep inside. Don't cry, he told himself. The tears came anyway. His face reddened with embarrassment. Why was he crying in front of this woman?

It's a powerful story, she said softly. His friends cried too. Their tears almost hid the real lesson. On life's journey, we pass guide-posts every day. Mostly we don't notice. Tragedy is the author of hope. Crisis brings us face to face with our soul.

Soul. Journey. He spoke deliberately, pondering each word. A year ago, I'd have been out of here.

And now?

Maybe I've met a new teacher.

Reclaiming Your Soul

It is by going into the abyss that we recover the treasures of life.

Where you stumble, there lies your treasure.

The very cave you are afraid to enter turns out to be the source of what you are looking for. The damned thing in the cave that was so dreaded has become the center. You find the jewel and it draws you off.

—Joseph Campbell

In their very first meeting, Maria invites Steve Camden to undertake a difficult journey, to plunge into his own personal abyss.
Sensibly enough, he hesitates. Does this "crazy woman" have any
idea what she is talking about? Will the cave he is afraid to enter
really bring him to what he is seeking? Or will that "damned
thing in the cave" simply bring more pain and confusion? Is this
trip necessary, or might it be a gigantic waste of time? Steve hopes
Maria will provide an itinerary and travel insurance before he
takes the plunge. She declines, knowing she can invite and
encourage but cannot tell him what will happen on his journey
or protect him from its rigors.

The malaise that has brought Steve Camden to Maria is widely
shared. He is suffering what Albert Schweitzer referred to as a
"sleeping sickness of the soul."[1] Its symptoms are loss of seri-
ousness, enthusiasm, and zest. When we live superficially, pur-
sue no goals deeper than material success, and never stop to
listen to our inner voices, we stunt our spiritual development.
Today's stressful and turbulent world compounds our risk of
shrunken souls and spiritual malaise. Technology, for all its won-
ders, makes it easier than ever for us to disconnect from ourselves
and others. Robert Putnam tells us that we too often wind up
"bowling alone," severed from family and community, because
we've substituted channel surfing for human engagement.[2]

Robert Lane marshals evidence of a long-term decline in happiness in prosperous democratic societies. He argues that more and more of us are misled by a materialist culture to put money and possessions at the center of our lives. We swallow the bait, ignoring the growing evidence that people who focus their lives on money are demonstrably less happy than people who strive for other, deeper purposes.[3]

The same restlessness and discontent inevitably leak into workplaces as well. Managers try almost anything to stay current and make their organizations successful. Sometimes their efforts pay off. Too often they and their organizations lose touch with their essence. This is true despite the growing evidence that companies with core beliefs and values that transcend the bottom line are, paradoxically, more profitable over time than companies that focus only on making money.[4] As consultants and researchers, we have repeatedly found that managers' first response to any situation is to focus on its rational and technical features. Analyze. Plan. Change policies. Restructure. Reengineer. For many business problems, these are sensible responses, but they miss another, deeper dimension. Our work has taught us that the symbolic, expressive facets of organizational life are at the heart of inspired leadership. Have we merely rediscovered *charisma,* the label often given to leaders endowed with mystery, magic, or a gift from the gods? Or are we seeing something more than that? Warren Buffett, one of America's most respected business leaders, once said that he looked for three qualities in new hires: integrity, intelligence, and energy. Hire someone without the first, he added, and the other two will kill you.[5] Integrity is rooted in identity and faith. That's one reason that spirit and soul are at the heart of the most successful leadership.

There is growing consensus that people today need a new paradigm to move beyond the traps of conventional thinking. In truth, we may need to rediscover and renew an old paradigm, one deeply embedded in traditional wisdom. Camden, this story's embattled leader, is lost. With the help of a spiritual guide, he is starting along another pathway. Instead of leading him to look outside for techniques and recipes, this path will teach him to look inward for a deeper source of wisdom. As John the Evangelist wrote to the early Christians about their understanding of Jesus, "The spirit you have received from him remains within you, and you don't need to have any man teach you. But that spirit teaches you all things and is the truth."[6] The same message is found in many other spiritual traditions. For example, it is told that in eighth-century China, a novice went to Ma-tzu, a spiritual master, in search of the Buddha's teaching. Ma-tzu asked him why he sought help from others when he already had the greatest treasure inside him. The novice asked what treasure Ma-tzu meant, and Ma-tzu replied: "Where is your question coming from? *This* is your treasure. It is precisely what is asking the question at this very moment. Everything is stored in this precious treasure-house of yours. It is there at your disposal, you can use it as you wish. Nothing is lacking. Why, then, are you running away from yourself and seeking for things outside?"[7]

The twenty-first-century milieu puts many obstacles in the way of this kind of journey to our spiritual center. Our pragmatic orientation places a premium on technical logic. Our tendency to specialize and compartmentalize leads us to dichotomize work and play, male and female, career and family, thinking and feeling, reason and spirit. We relegate spirituality to churches, temples, and mosques—for those who still attend them. We shun it at work. To change this way of thinking is far from easy, but more and more people are recognizing the costs of this separation. One of the principal findings of Mitroff and Denton's landmark study of spirituality in the workplace was that *"people do not want to compartmentalize or fragment their lives. The search for meaning, purpose, wholeness, and integration is a constant, never-ending task. To confine this search to one day a week or after hours violates people's basic sense of integrity, of being whole persons. In short, soul is not something one leaves at home."*[8]

Steve is now on the verge of a perilous existential journey that can take him to his soul. Early on, he will rely heavily on Maria, his spiritual guide, for support and direction. Yet she will resist his efforts to put her in charge. Instead, she affirms a message found in almost every spiritual tradition: Don't try to put someone else in charge of your spiritual journey. Instead, recognize and trust the power within you.

Steve will learn that his task is to *re*claim and *re*kindle his spiritual center. What he needs to find is already within him because spirit is unquenchable. "It does not matter how long your spirit lies dormant and unused. One day you hear a song, look at an object, or see a vision and you feel its presence. It can't be bought, traded, or annihilated, because its power comes from its story. No one can steal your spirit. You have to give it away. You can also take it back."[9] Yet taking it back is rarely easy. Steve is embarking on a voyage that he has avoided for many years.

Steve's quest will be filled with paradox. "Spirituality transcends the ordinary; and yet, paradoxically, it can be found only in the ordinary. Spirituality is *beyond* us and yet is in everything we do. It is extraordinary, and yet it is extraordinarily simple."[10]

Another paradox is that the specifics of each person's journey can never be forecast even though the journey's outlines are known to us all because this quest is the most often told tale in all human cultures. Consider a pair of examples—one very old and one very new.

Beowulf is one of the oldest surviving works in English literature. It is the story of a prince, Beowulf, who establishes his leadership by courageously going forth to confront and destroy a murderous beast, Grendel. Beowulf soon learns the price of victory: he must face Grendel's vicious and vengeful mother in her den at the bottom of an icy pond. The English poet David Whyte has explored the spiritual message in the story. In going to the depths to confront Grendel's mother, Whyte tells us, Beowulf is in quest of his own soul. Symbolically, Grendel's mother represents the beast within himself that Beowulf must face and conquer if he is to know himself and to grow.[11]

More than a thousand years later, J. K. Rowland has created a publishing sensation with a series of novels, ostensibly for children, about a boy wizard named Harry Potter. In each of the first two novels in the series, the climax comes as Harry confronts his own Grendel's mother in the form of different personifications of the evil Lord Voldemort (whose French name means "flight of death"). Each time, the confrontation requires that Harry plunge courageously down into the depths of subterranean passages and caverns. Like Beowulf, Harry carries the reader in search of his and their souls.

Neither Potter nor Beowulf is foolish enough to go on his quest alone. Beowulf is aided by loyal retainers. Harry is supported by two faithful friends. The challenges and dangers of the spiritual journey are so great that few are likely to succeed without help. Steve Camden will need the guide he has found in Maria to support him along the way. As authors, neither of us could have written *Leading with Soul* alone. We needed each other's support as we sought our own spiritual centers.

In *Beowulf,* the Harry Potter novels, and the countless other variations on the story of spiritual development, the hero's journey typically moves through three major stages. The first stage is leaving home—often physically but especially psychically and spiritually. Leaving home requires letting go of comfortable and familiar ways. It makes it possible to escape the shackles of established convention and everyday routine. In his very first meeting with Maria, Steve begins to take this initial step—letting go of the old psychic anchors and entrenched defenses that had locked him into a particular way of thinking about himself and his life. As is often the case in such journeys, Steve leaves home not because he wants to but because he has to. He has hit a brick wall—his old patterns and assumptions have been failing him. He has tried to get around the wall by doing more of what he knows, but that has also failed. Because home has become intolerable, Steve is willing to risk embarking on a new journey.

Leaving home leads to the journey's second stage—the quest. The quest is always a time of almost overwhelming danger and challenge. Beowulf and Potter both narrowly avert death. Steve, like most modern managers, faces only trivial physical dangers. But he correctly recognizes that the psychological and spiritual stakes are very high. That is why his initial impulse is to reject the journey—to "get away from this crazy woman." That urge will return from time to time, because the quest always has peaks and valleys. But if he persists and enters the last stage of the journey, he will develop and deepen in ways that could never happen otherwise. As Joseph Campbell said: "The dark night of the soul comes just before revelation. When everything is lost, and all seems darkness, then comes the new life and all that is needed."[12] Only then will Steve Camden be ready for the third stage of the journey, returning home. Home will be different and so will he, because he will be armed with new capacities and the deeper understanding that he could acquire only by undertaking this journey. But at the moment, most of the adventure still lies ahead for Steve Camden. Like Beowulf and Harry Potter, he will find that reclaiming his soul requires uncommon courage and persistence.

Conviction

CHAPTER 5

A Place to Start

A month passed. He was back on her doorstep. Waiting again. His shoulders were slumped, his expression dour. He felt his heart pounding. Where was she? Why was he back? Something had pulled him. But what? Then she was there. He felt better. At least she hadn't deserted him.

She led him to her study. Motioned him to a chair. He sat down. Groped for words.

How are you doing? she asked.

Looking for insights. Waiting for a light bulb to go on.

And?

Nothing. Darkness. More confused than ever. He looked down. He felt stupid.

That's good.

He was surprised again. Why?

You've begun your journey. At the start, confusion is to be expected.

But I feel lost.

You want everything planned in advance. That's fine for a trip to Chicago. It won't work for a journey of the spirit. First, you have to get started. Move into uncharted territory. Explore. Meditate. You'll know if you're on course.

How will I know? It feels scary.

Why? she asked.

Memories from childhood for one thing. I got lost at a carnival once. I was panicked. Terrified. I still dream about it. Remember Hansel and Gretel? In new places, I still leave crumbs.

She was smiling broadly. Almost beaming.

What's so funny? he asked.

I'm smiling because your story is so familiar. As a little girl, I used to play in a field next to our house. It was very hot one summer. Everything was very dry. I built a campfire. It jumped over the ring of rocks. The whole field caught fire. It took the fire department two hours to put it out. I felt stupid. For a long time, I was terrified of doing the wrong thing again. I tried to avoid anything risky.

That's not what I've heard about you.

I've learned on my journey. I wanted to find courage—like the Cowardly Lion in *The Wizard of Oz*. The Wizard says that everyone is afraid. Courage is the ability to go on anyway. It took me a long time, but I've learned to go on.

I want you to be the wizard. Give me the answers. You keep telling me to look inside. When I do, I hear the same voices. Be rational. Be in control. Be careful.

Those are messages from your head, not from your heart. It's hard to let go of old rules. It takes courage and faith.

Where do I find them?

You keep looking.

Where?

You've asked that question before. Let's try a different way. She stood up. She waved him over to a window. Those woods

go on for miles. Take a walk. Get off the path. Explore. Make sure of one thing. Get lost.

Get lost? He stared at her in disbelief.

Exactly. Try it. See what happens.

I already know. I panic.

You think you know. You might discover something else. In the legend of the Holy Grail, each knight began his search by entering the darkest place in the forest. No path. No guide. Try it.

He started toward the door. He hesitated. Old fears pulled at him. He turned around, smiled. Any crumbs to drop along the way?

They both laughed as he headed out the door.

CHAPTER 6

Vicissitudes of the Journey

It was getting dark. He was still lost, scrambling down a brushy slope. He never saw the branch until it slapped him in the face. It stung. His eyes watering, he sat down. He fought the panic. Old memories swept over him. His father's death. His mother's breakdown. Living with grandparents. Working his way through college. Vowing to be successful. Getting what he wanted. Finding that it only brought more worries.

Much later, he was back at her house, enjoying the aroma of fresh coffee.

I was about to mount a search party. She smiled. Was she amused? Or relieved?

You told me to get lost. I did.

Do you ever do anything halfway? Then she noticed the blood.
What happened?

Close encounter with a tree. It won.

Here. Let's clean it off.

It's nothing.

Sit down! She spoke sternly. I'll be back in a minute.

He protested weakly. She ignored him and washed the scrape.
Her touch was gentler than he expected. Close, her eyes were
brighter, deeper. Like peering into a surging seascape. The feelings were almost too intense. He looked away.

Found a lake, he said. He was trying to change the subject.
Walked around it a couple of times. Ran into more than the
branch. Discovered things I buried long ago.

You can learn a lot walking around a lake.

When you were young, did you learn a prayer, 'Now I lay me
down to sleep?—'

She interrupted. 'I pray the Lord my soul to keep.'

The next lines terrified me. 'If I should die before I wake, / I
pray the Lord my soul to take.' Particularly after my father died.

Do you still pray?

Not for years.

Why not?

Never seemed to make a difference. I stopped believing.

What do you believe in now?

I don't know. Maybe myself. Maybe nothing. He sounded resigned.

When you don't know what you believe in, you don't know who you are. You have no idea why you're here. You can't see where you're going. She spoke slowly, quietly. Every word emphasized.

I used to know where I was going. I got lost somehow.

Prayer is an avenue to faith. It's an intimate conversation with your soul. A heartsong.

A heartsong?

Your heart knows things that your mind can't. Everyone needs a heartsong. It sustains you through the vicissitudes of the journey.

Vicissitudes? When had he last heard that word? In church? In the back of his mind a distant echo. She continued.

A spiritual pilgrimage always brings peaks and valleys. A heartsong sustains you along the way.

I remember sitting with my mother in a black church. Music and singing. So much energy and intensity. Joy in the room. But spirituals are about suffering as well as happiness. They're a way to survive the pain.

Heartsongs carry us through both exhilaration and heartache. You've etherized your life to avoid the pain. At a price. If you wall off the valleys, you close off the peaks as well. It's better to stop and sing from time to time.

Ether. Pain. More memories. His divorce. His children's suffering. An older son who never forgave him. The feelings would wait no longer.

He felt her touch.

Fifteen years since my divorce, he said. My oldest son still doesn't answer my letters. The pain never stopped.

What did you do with it?

Ignored it. Threw myself into my work.

Did you talk to anyone?

A counselor. Nothing much happened. I was trying to get to something. Something deeper. I never found it.

Good counselors know the psyche. Great ones know the soul. People used to go to their priest or rabbi for spiritual guidance. Now where do they go?

Nowhere, I guess. Try to bury the feelings. Like I did.

Your divorce wounded your spirit. It's still not healed.

Is healing possible?

Yes. It's not easy, but it's possible.

How?

Tragedy enters every life. Spirit springs from what you make of it. Wounds provide an eye to find new possibilities.

He knew she was right. He remembered a story. I had a friend who wanted to be a champion rock climber. He got trapped in the mountains for a couple of days. Frostbite. Both legs amputated below the knee. He was determined to climb again. He got artificial limbs for climbing. Someone asked him how he could climb so well. He laughed. He said now his calves didn't cramp.

Humor is a wonderful heartsong, isn't it?

I need to find my own.

Leaning into Your Fear

A good traveler has no fixed plans and is not intent upon arriving. A good artist lets his intuition lead him wherever it wants. A good scientist has freed himself of concepts and keeps his mind open to what is.

—Lao-tzu

Images of Leadership

Steve seeks help when he becomes desperate. He hopes for specific solutions to immediate concerns. He resists seeing that outward problems are only symptoms of something much deeper. Slowly, he begins to see that his real challenge is to come to terms with his soul. Maria becomes his guide.

Steve has bought the widespread misconception that leadership expresses itself through individual heroism—waging war, championing a great cause, or single-handedly changing the course of history. In this view, which has been especially attractive to men, leaders' success or failure is of their own making. They succeed if they have the right stuff—strength, courage, and vision. Failure is proof of their personal deficiencies. A familiar archetypal image of the hero is the autonomous, lonely individual wandering on the fringes of society—the Lone Ranger, Dirty Harry, or Rambo. This view taints our images of leadership. Would-be heroes pay a heavy personal price: alienation, feelings of failure, stress-induced illness, and early death. Organizations and institutions suffer and sputter because we ask too much of our leaders and too little of ourselves.

Leadership is a relationship rooted in community. Leaders embody their group's most precious values and beliefs. Their ability to lead emerges from the strength and sustenance of those around them. It persists and deepens as they learn to use life's wounds to discover their own spiritual centers. As they conquer the demons within, they achieve the inner peace and bedrock confidence that enable them to inspirit and inspire others.

Finding One's Spiritual Center

The spiritual journey that leaders must take, and inspire others to take, begins *with* ourselves but not necessarily *by* ourselves. Maria tells Steve to look both inside and outside because his quest will require both an internal exploration of soul and an external search for communion. To aid in the journey inward, every religious tradition has developed spiritual disciplines, or exercises, for getting in touch with something bigger. One is prayer, the *heartsong* that Maria offered to Steve. As the Ulanows have observed, "Prayer is primary speech. [It] starts without words and often ends without them. . . . It works some of the time in signs and symbols, lurches when it must, leaps when it can, has several kinds of logic at its disposal."[1] Other spiritual practices include meditating, studying scriptures, singing hymns, following prescribed rituals, journeying to sacred places, and contemplating nature. Similar practices have evolved independently in many different places and eras. There is a meditative tradition, for example, in almost every major religion, including Buddhism, Christianity, Hinduism, Islam, and Judaism.

The external journey is a search for collective spirit, for true community with others. Steve has found a spiritual guide. He might have drawn support from a circle of friends, a spouse, close colleagues, or a religious community. But whatever our external source of support, the first step toward enlightenment is an exploration of our inner being, a search for our spiritual center. Only then can we lead others. "In the end, it is not our techniques, our talents or our knowledge that matter, it is our being."[2] As Gandhi put it, we must "become the change that we want to see in the world."[3]

Steve is learning to confront his fears—of letting go, of being out of control, of losing contact with comforting habitual anchors. He is embracing an ancient spiritual maxim: to hold too tightly to anything is to lose everything. As a seventh-century Zen master said: "The Great Way isn't difficult for those who are unattached to their preferences. Let go of longing and aversion, and everything will be perfectly clear."[4] William Blake said it another way:

He who binds himself to a joy
Does the wingèd life destroy;
But he who kisses the joy as it flies
Lives in eternity's sunrise.[5]

Steve's conversations with Maria are helping him find the determination to move on. He cannot know in advance where his quest will lead. The decision to begin and the conviction to persevere must rest on faith in the groping rather than fore-knowledge of the grasp. The journey begins only when Steve's heart tells him that this is what he must do—even if reason and logic tell him otherwise. As he listens to his heartsong and finds the courage to answer its call, he embarks on an odyssey. As he continues, he will see things once invisible and do things once impossible.

Steve has lived his life in a safe zone, hoping to minimize uncertainty and to avoid pain. He is beginning to see that his safe haven was a spiritual prison. "It is in passionate leaps of faith that we propel the human spirit forward. The safety of the known which only leads to boredom stifles the experience of life. As with heroes everywhere, the course of our lives may become a beacon to others who are on their own quests."[6]

History is full of stories of common people who do extraordinary things. In surmounting anguish and pain they kindle their spirits and give strength to others. Modern society encourages people to follow recipes or consult experts rather than find the fortitude to look inward. We buy diet books as a substitute for losing weight. We buy self-help books as an alternative to confronting our deepest fears and imperfections. We move from fad to fad without putting our heart fully into anything. We feel powerless in the face of the many social and organizational ills. Beneath our helplessness is a spiritual vacuum. It saps our faith, weakens our hearts, and leaves us foundering.

Spirit and Imperfection

Bill Irwin provides one example of what uncommon spirit can do. Excessive drinking left him blind by age twenty-eight. In his early fifties, a recovering alcoholic, he decided to hike the entire 2,167 miles of the Appalachian Trail. His Seeing Eye dog was his sole companion. He faced daunting hazards: cliffs, storms, biting insects, and his own fear. Before starting, he committed himself to the journey: "I don't care how many times I fall, I can always crawl to Maine."[7] Eight months later, he became the first blind man to walk the length of the trail.

How did he do it? "He never saw the trail. He just took it. He did not stick to the plan others preconceived for the life of a blind man. He sought his own course, the one his spirit needed to follow."[8]

Embedded in Bill Irwin's story are the dual messages of human imperfection and human transcendence. Irwin's youthful imperfection led to his blindness. But he embraced a maxim that offers an alternative to the shallow optimism of the 1960s and the deep pessimism of the 1980s and 1990s. It says, "I'm not OK, and you're not OK. But that's all right."[9]

Paradoxically, in accepting our imperfections, we develop the conviction needed to embark on an ill-defined search for a better place. We also realize that the end of one quest is a prologue to the next. Ernest Becker, author of the Pulitzer Prize–winning book *The Denial of Death,* observes that "man is the God who shits."[10] That paradox cuts to the heart of spirituality. To deny imperfections is to deny our humanity and to become disconnected from our soul. The leader who falters, like the God who shits, is a paradox that only spirit enables us to accept and embrace. A preacher once asked a group of children, "If all the good people in the world were red and all the bad people were green, what color would you be?" One girl thought for a long time, looking very serious. Then her face brightened, and she said, "Reverend, I'd be streaky."[11]

We're all streaky. Acceptance of fear and imperfection and a willingness to undertake the journey anyway transport us to life's deepest core, "the inner value, the rapture that is associated with being alive."[12]

Gifts

CHAPTER 7

Gifts of Leadership

Late November. Gloomy sky. Chilling rain. As he trudged up the path, he could see her watching him through the window. His pace was brisk. His face told another story. Frustration. Gloom. Something unfinished.

After brief pleasantries, she got to the point. You seem disappointed.

Yes and no. Ups and downs. Sometimes I'm soaring. It's like a great adventure. Mistakes don't drag me down so much. You were right about prayer. It helps.

You're finding heartsongs.

Particularly from Gwen.

Gwen is special to you?

I've asked her to marry me.

Has she agreed?

Not yet. But she's got me going to church on alternate Sundays. I'd been away too long. I'd forgotten the power. The prayers. The music. The liturgy. The feeling of community.

What about the other Sundays?

We take walks around a lake. We talk. We listen to the wind in the trees. Lunch in the same meadow each time. If you look, you find reverence in nature.

She nodded.

He scanned the room. Suddenly it hit him.

No photos, he said.

What?

No photos. First time I came, I knew something was missing. Beautiful art. But no friends. No family. No people.

He thought he saw something different in her eyes. Turmoil? Sadness? Quickly it was gone.

The art is enough, she said.

Was she telling the truth? Hiding something? Was he too intrusive? Avoiding his own struggles?

72

She moved on, ignoring his unstated question. You were saying mistakes don't bother you as much.

He suspected she was changing the subject. But why? He decided to let it go.

Not as much. I'm clearer about what's important. But it's hard to express.

Why?

When I mention spirit, other people look at me like I'm an alien.

Everyone?

Not Gwen. She understands. So do a few friends. No one at work.

What happens there?

I'm their boss. They're careful. I can feel it. See it in their eyes. I've been trying to drum up support for a weekly 'spirit breakfast.' Right now, I'm not sure anyone would come. I feel like a band leader who turned left at a fork. The rest of the band turned right.

You're trying to lead, but no one's following.

A drum major strutting solo.

Steve, you're discovering one of life's most precious gifts—the treasure of human spirit. You need to share it. You lead with soul by giving it to others.

Leaders are supposed to give direction.

What if I had directed you to seek your soul?

He paused, taking a moment to cover his embarrassment. I'd have left. I wanted to anyway. Maybe it's the same with people in my organization. Sharing spirit sounds good. But how?

With gifts.

Gifts?

Look at any of the great spiritual traditions. You find two moral precepts at the core. Compassion. Justice. Are they at the heart of your organization?

I wish they were.

You can build them through your gifts.

What gifts?

Ultimately you have to discover your own gifts.

Have you found yours?

I've found four in particular. They emerge from two basic dualities: yin and yang, matter and spirit.

Dualities? He felt skeptical.

Opposites that make each other possible.

What was she talking about? Like without pain there is no joy?

That's it. Opposites in harmony. The four gifts provide balance.

No question, my organization could use some balance. But how?

From yin, the female principle, caring and compassion—the gift of love. From yang, the male principle, autonomy and influence—the gift of power. From matter, the pragmatic world, accomplishment and craftsmanship—the gift of authorship.

And the fourth?

Later. When you're ready.

He felt a surge of anger. Come on! Was he a child? He didn't need to be spoon-fed.

She sensed his anger. Impatience only slows your journey, she said.

She's been right before, he told himself.

All right. Tell me about authorship.

It's the feeling of putting your own signature on your work. It's the sheer joy of creating something of lasting value. The feeling of adding something special to our world.

That's where I've been concentrating. We've been pushing hard on our World-Class Quality program. Getting our people focused on excellence. Producing something they can be proud of.

Are you satisfied with the results?

Not really. The harder I push, the more they seem to push back.

You see the paradox? You hope they will become what you think they are not. You're trying to get them to accept something that you don't think they want.

I'm just trying to motivate them to do their best. Isn't that leadership?

Do you motivate a rosebush to blossom? Can you impel your children to grow? When you push someone to become what she's already becoming, you get in the way. You become a meddler.

He felt the blood rise to his face. His throat tightened. His voice rose.

Didn't you just say to give people authorship? That's precisely what I'm trying to do! How else am I supposed to get them to set higher standards?

Why do Zen masters teach that if you meet the Buddha on the road, kill him?

His brow knitted in puzzlement. Why did she keep answering questions with questions? What was she trying to tell him? He looked down at the floor. He looked for a connection. Finally it came.

Because answers aren't outside. They're inside. I'm asking you when I already know the answer. He glanced out the window. The weather is lousy. Still, a good time for a walk.

He started down the steps. Still raining. Cold. Windy. Should he turn around? No, he'd feel foolish. And he wanted time to himself. He closed his raincoat and plunged forward.

Authorship

He cut the walk short. Too cold.

She handed him a drink. Here's something to take the chill off.

The fifth gift—coffee, he replied.

She laughed. He sipped the dark brew. No cranes. Just a simple beige mug.

You were right, he said.

About what?

Shipping my question back to me, he continued. I wanted you to do my work. You wouldn't. I had to create my own composition.

Did you succeed?

I realized something. I was doing to you what people at work do to me.

What's that?

Upward delegation. Dumping stuff in my lap.

Why?

Collusion. I love being the guy who solves the tough problems. They know I love it. They give me what I want.

It's a great way for you to stay busy.

Swamped. With everyone else's work. They're off the hook. Protected from mistakes. And from learning. Meanwhile, I never have time for the big picture.

It's the curse of the American leader. Particularly for men.

What curse? A trace of annoyance. Is male bashing part of the program?

No. But rugged individualism is deep in the American psyche. Remember Gary Cooper in *High Noon*? The leader saves the day all by himself while the townspeople cower in the background. It's an endemic cultural message: 'If you have a problem, hope for a hero to rescue you.'

And blame the hero if things don't work out, he added. We're not responsible. It's the leader's job to solve our problems.

It's sometimes different in Japan, she said. There, it's the group's job to solve the leader's problems.

I had a similar thought on my walk. I read once about two oil company executives. Both had the same problem—a fire in a refinery. The American executive got a call at home. Rushed in. Met with his people. Got reports from the scene. Gave orders. A frantic morning of fire fighting.

A lovely example of the American way.

The Japanese executive arrived in his office. He sipped a cup of tea. Relaxed. Read the newspaper. Reviewed reports. Thought about strategy in the Middle East. Learned about the fire after it was under control. Subordinates explained how they had handled it. He congratulated them.

That executive understands something about the gift of authorship.

And he probably enjoys life more than I do. I always thought I was good at delegating. Clear about expectations. Good follow-up. But the buck still stops with me.

So your people don't feel a sense of authorship.

Hell, no. They're always looking over their shoulders. Trying to figure out what I want. Then I complain that they don't take responsibility. Vicious cycle.

Where no one wins.

If they succeed, I take credit. If they fail, I blame them. The crazy thing is that I put in a motivation program. Trying to persuade them of what they probably want to do anyway—if I'd just get out of the way.

It's a classic pattern. You're the parent and they're the kids. You shield them from responsibility. They look to you for direction and security.

They know I have the final say. Review everything they do. Why give me their best? They know I'll change it anyway.

You got a lot done on a short walk. She was smiling.

More than you think. I jumped ahead. Started to think about the gift of love.

How far did you get?

Not very. Stayed close to home. Started with Gwen. I love her. I know that deep in my heart. I wish I could express it better. I need to understand love as a gift.

What's happening with you and Gwen?

Good things. But hard to talk about. Why was she asking? She must have a reason. She always did.

I'm glad. Keep giving. You'll learn with practice.

And if I meet the Buddha?

Love him. You're making headway, she laughed. You may not even need me much longer. She walked him to the door.

He said good-bye. He wanted to say more. Why did she say he might not need her? Was she pushing him away? He didn't want that. Not yet.

CHAPTER 9

Love

It was February. Freezing. A driving rain beat against his windshield. The forecast promised snow in the mountains. He liked driving in snow. It softened things. Nothing to interrupt his solitude. A chance to think.

He thought about love. What made that word so powerful? He could talk about love with Gwen. Sometimes with his children. Never at work. Who talks about love in a corporation? You talk about it at weddings. Six months until the wedding. Gwen had finally said yes. Maybe the only love he really felt sure about.

Two months until his trip to Singapore. A new acquisition there. Great company. A merger is a little like a wedding, he thought. Two different companies. We can learn from them if we don't strangle them. That's the danger: we own you, so do it our way.

That's the connection. Same problem with Gwen. They had their biggest fights when he tried to make her more like him. Yet he loved her because she wasn't like him. Loving her meant treasuring who she is. The same with the acquisition. It's got to be mutual.

Whiteout. Snow so heavy he couldn't see past the wipers. He pulled off the road. Turned off the ignition. Silence. He *loved* nights like this. But the gift of love is something deeper. More spiritual. He smiled at the thought of spirit. It wouldn't have occurred to him before he met Maria.

He heard snowplows. Droning. Clanking. As they passed, he pulled in behind.

Well after midnight, he arrived at her home. The snow had stopped. The sky was clearing quickly. He saw a light in her study. She was waiting. He had hoped she would be.

He paused to look at the night sky. Dark patches of clouds giving way to stars. The moon almost full. In the past on nights like this, the sky spoke of cosmic comedy. Tonight it spoke to him of love.

You must be exhausted, she called from the front porch.

He was surprised. A departure from the routine. He wouldn't have to wait for her to come to the door.

Physically, yes, he called back. Spiritually, never better.

He came in. A mug of coffee was waiting.

I was starting to worry, she said.

No need. I've been driving in snow a long time. Had to stop once. Almost a total whiteout. Couldn't see a thing.

What did you do?

Pulled off. Watched the snow. Thought about love.

What happened?

A team of snowplows came along. I followed them.

That wasn't my question.

I know. He looked at her. You've given me love since the first time we met.

He wasn't prepared for her reaction. She glanced away momentarily, but said nothing.

He contin-
ued. I didn't
understand love.
I thought it was
just attraction
and desire.
Like a business
deal: you invest in the
hope of a big return.
That's not it.

She stood up. Let's talk more tomorrow. Even if you're not tired, I am. If you're hungry, try your luck in the refrigerator. How about we meet at eight?

He nodded assent.

We'll take a walk before breakfast, she added. It should be beautiful. She turned away.

See you in the morning, he responded.

He was puzzled. When he mentioned love, she seemed to pull back. He poured more coffee. He wandered around the house. All this art. No photos of people. She's always intense, but always composed. What's behind her mask? Is she afraid of something? Is that why she lives up here alone?

By morning, the sunlight dazzled in the new snow. Maria was her usual self. Warm. Confident. Inscrutable. He wanted to ask about last night. He decided to start on safer ground.

How do I give love in my organization? he asked as they walked along.

She smiled. He watched her breath form a translucent cloud in the icy air. Jesus washed the feet of his disciples shortly before his death. He told them to follow his example.

How do you do that in a business?

There are Japanese executives who spend time every week cleaning toilets. It's part of their gift.

I'd try it, but people are already looking at me a little funny.

How *do* people know you care? she asked.

They don't. Particularly now. We had to lay people off last month.

How did you do it?

We did everything. Gave them plenty of notice. Supervisors met with everyone who was affected. We paid for counseling. Hired an outplacement service.

Did you talk to them yourself? she asked.

No. They're three or four levels down. Most of them I don't know.

Aren't you their leader?

He paused and scanned the snow-covered landscape. You see the branches sinking under the weight of the snow? he asked.

Yes.

That's how I feel at work. Drooping under the burden. Like I've given all I can. There's not enough to go around.

You've got it turned around, she said. Maybe you're burdened because you haven't given enough.

Not as much as the Japanese executives. By that standard, I haven't shown people that I care about them.

Do they care about you? she asked.

Never really thought about it. Caring about the boss isn't in the job description.

Do you think love is a one-way street? Why didn't you talk to the people who were laid off? Look them in the eye. Give them comfort. Show them you understood.

I was busy, he protested halfheartedly. I didn't want to undermine the chain of command.

Those sound like lousy reasons.

OK. Maybe I was afraid to face them. So I let someone else do it.

If you show people you don't care, they'll return the favor. Show them you care about them, they might surprise you.

An old message. When you give love, you get it back. But I'm not sure I believe it.

A lot of people don't. They usually don't know what they're missing. The costs are subtle.

Such as?

Disconnection. Wondering why you can't get through to people.

Like me when I first came to see you.

Exactly. But when people know someone really cares, you can see it. It's there in their faces. And in their actions. Love really does keep on giving.

The opening he was looking for. Then why, he asked, did you reject my gift last night?

I was touched, but I wasn't expecting it. Maybe you were offering me something I wasn't ready for just then.

Was I getting too close?

No, but maybe you were moving too fast. I think it was the timing.

Timing. An old lesson. Always in a hurry. He'd tried to rush her. Pin her down. She wasn't rejecting his offer. But she wouldn't be caught up in his urgency. He had more to learn.

He thought back to his organization. With the people we laid off, I missed the moment. But I can still do something with the people who stayed. I need to get out to Topeka. Singapore too. I'm learning how to give authorship. But I'm not sure where to begin with love.

Remember that everyone's different. A big part of love is caring enough to find out what really matters to others.

I haven't been doing that enough. Not last night. Not in my organization. I need to.

What's holding you back?

Fear, mostly.

Of what?

Of getting too close. Of opening my heart to people around me. Can they know me too well? Will they lose respect?

How could you test whether those fears are justified?

I don't think I'll clean the office toilets tomorrow. But I'll find my own way.

CHAPTER 10

Power

A dazzling spring day. More than a year since they first met. Perennials lining the way to her door. He laughed as he remembered his first visit. The fear and confusion he'd brought with him. Nothing like the joy he felt at seeing her again.

How was Singapore? she asked.

Tough. Even tougher than I expected. But it came out all right.

What happened?

I tried to show them I cared. My gift of love.

Were they looking for that?

No. Not at first. Lots of polite smiles. But you could feel the chill. They had a reception. I gave a little speech. I talked about caring. It flopped.

How could you tell?

Arms crossed, blank faces everywhere.

Then what happened?

I went out on the factory floor. One of the workers, a young guy with a big, earnest smile, asked me to take a turn on his machine. I didn't have much choice. Big crowd circled around. I felt like a lamb circled by hungry wolves. I was fumbling all over the place. I probably turned out 100 percent scrap. People thought it was hilarious.

And they loved you for it?

Just being out on the floor was the big thing. Talking to people. Saying hello. Answering questions. I think I passed a test. On the way out, I met this woman. Maybe fifty years old, Chinese, tough looking. Came up and threw her arms around me. Told me everyone figured all I cared about was money. 'Now,' she says, 'we have a friend in America.'

How did you feel?

When a factory worker in Singapore gives you a hug, that's pretty amazing.

Love only works when people feel it and believe it. She smiled. Groups create testing grounds. They're like sacred spaces, but most of the time we don't even know they're there. When you're in one and you give from your heart, people know it's real.

Whatever worked in Singapore backfired in Topeka.

What happened there?

Timing was bad. Six months after the layoffs. I knew it would be tough. But I worked in Topeka my first job out of college. I thought we were still family.

A risky assumption.

I found that out. There's this big guy, looks like he could have been a linebacker in the NFL. Runs a forklift. Abrasive as hell. Anyway, as soon as I get there, he's in my face, screaming. I'd fired his friends. He tells me I'm a phony, pretending we're one big happy family. Like all those other big shots with big salaries.

That must have stung.

Worse than that tree limb. Torture. You know how it feels, hanging out there?

I've been there. I still have the scars.

It got worse. They knew how to twist the knife. End of the day, I was battered. Sat in the hotel room, nursing a glass of wine. Feeling sorry for myself. Wondering where I could hide. Just wanting out of there.

That's when you called me, isn't it? You woke me up.

It wasn't that late. I thought you'd be awake.

I wasn't feeling well that evening. I was tired.

I'll call earlier next time. Are you OK?

There's a lot of stuff going around this year.

You helped me see that I'd brought the wrong gift. Bad timing again. I was offering love. They were saying bullshit, why'd you fire our friends? They weren't looking for caring. Not from me anyway. They wanted power.

She laughed. You dug yourself in pretty deep. Did you ever get out?

Not before I ate a lot of dirt. Next day we had this meeting. Old conference room in the plant. Cramped, bare walls, fluorescents, Formica table, plastic chairs. Martha Mendez, the union head, and her executive committee on one side of the table. Me and the plant manager on the other. They're mad. I'm scared. Mendez lays it all out. Rakes me and management over the coals. I'm biting my tongue so hard it bleeds.

It sounds pretty brutal. Have your wounds healed?

They're better. I sat there. Listened, asked questions. Told them I got the message. They felt

betrayed. We'd been talking about listening, participation, empowerment for a long time. Then when something big comes along we get amnesia. 'You admit you blew it?' Mendez asks.

How did you respond?

I choked on the words, but I said yes.

You were pretty far out on a limb.

Fifty feet above a rock quarry and she was revving up her chain saw. I promised two things. Next time, I said, we'll listen. And we'll work with you to make this plant successful.

Layoffs are bad for credibility. Did they believe you?

No, not at first. But a couple of weeks later I got invited back. Some workers and managers had banded together to develop some proposals. They'd done their homework. Gathered data. Called other plants. Worked through some conflict. Agreed on what needed to be done. Some of it needed help from head-quarters. Another test, I guess. I almost flunked.

How?

One guy in the group threw a half-baked idea in the hopper. No way we could spend that kind of money without a more careful look. I almost told him flat out it was a dumb idea. I bit my tongue and thought hard. Then I asked him to lead a group to study it further. He was proud.

It sounds like a good move. Caving in doesn't empower people. You set a good example. You went to the plant. You listened. You were open.

Some of their ideas were terrific. Easy to say yes to. That night, Mendez invited me over to her house for barbecue. The whole union executive committee was there. Best team-building session I ever saw.

What did you learn?

You can give power away and wind up with more. You remember the old gasoline ad? I always thought power was like the tiger in the tank. You don't want to let the tiger out, you just let people hear him roar.

Hoard power, dampen spirit.

That's what I learned in Topeka.

CHAPTER 11

Significance

He was surprised, troubled when she opened the door. The gray in her hair and lines in her face had always been there. But not the first thing you noticed. Was she tired? Sick? Her face gave no other clue. Her eyes and her smile were as mysterious as ever.

She motioned him in. There's hot coffee.

He thanked her. Notice the headline this morning? Another young movie star dead. ODed on drugs.

She nodded. She seemed to understand. Why didn't he?

How can you have it all and have nothing? he asked.

Do you remember yourself when we first met?

Was she baiting another hook? She kept him alert, anyway. Forced him to think.

You're right. The higher I climbed, the less it meant.

You felt insignificant.

Meaning what?

Meaning you were hollow at the core. No soul, no spirit, nothing.

How about some credit for progress?

Do you want to talk about the past or the future?

Maria, you are the most demanding, infuriating—

She interrupted and gestured toward the door. It caught him by surprise. You called this meeting. You can leave whenever you want.

Leave! I just drove three hours to get here. He paused and laughed at himself. Not even an E for effort?

She laughed too. She must have known how he would react. How's your spirit? she asked. Her tone was gentler.

I remember the first time you asked. I figured you weren't playing with a full deck. It didn't make any sense. Now it makes a lot.

You've made progress. But something else is on your mind.

The fourth gift. You never told me what it was.

I don't need to. You already know.

And?

What were we just talking about?

About how infuriating you are.

Before that, remember?

The movie star who died. Having it all and having nothing. Feeling insignificant.

Why not start there? she asked.

I did feel insignificant. Not now. Things make more sense. He paused, grasping for the right word. Significance! That's what the fourth gift is about. Why hadn't he seen that before? Then it hit him. That's what you've given me.

Now you can give it to others.

How?

Do you want me to do your work? You know about authorship. It's your organization. What comes to mind?

Times when I've felt significant. Maybe what works for me will apply to my organization.

Keep going.

Like my visit to Singapore. It was like being present at a birth. Coming together to generate something new. The power of shared emotion. Creating a common spirit that touched everyone.

How did it happen?

Maybe magic. Maybe love. I'm not sure. We prepared—a lot. Everyone knew the script, even though it wasn't written down. It still felt very spontaneous.

That's how good rituals feel.

Bad ones can backfire, though. My lesson in Topeka began as a disaster. I thought I was Santa Claus bringing gifts. They thought I was Scrooge blowing away their friends.

What did you learn from that experience?

You can't impose significance. People have to create it together.

Exactly. Significance comes from working with others, doing something worth doing, making the world better. After that, you confirm the feeling and deepen it.

How?

With celebrations.

Celebrations?

Memorable events for special occasions. Holiday parties. Summer picnics. Annual sales meetings. Quarterly off-site retreats. They can all connect people to a deeper, spiritual world.

He looked skeptical. We have a holiday party every December. Plenty of spirits. But not much spirit.

Then you're missing an opportunity. When you do them well, celebrations weave hearts and souls into a shared destiny. People have always summoned spirit by coming together to mark beginnings and endings, triumphs and tragedies, births and deaths.

We probably don't do that enough in my business.

Nor in most. So you lose the spiritual glue that holds people together. Think about religion. What are the ties there that bond people to one another?

He thought for a while. You know the Emerald Buddha? he finally asked.

In Bangkok. I remember it vividly.

The faithful come to pray every day. The King of Thailand visits three times a year to change the Buddha's clothes. Fit the costume to the season.

A place of great reverence, she said.

Like the Cathedral of Notre-Dame in Paris. I remember standing there once in awe. The architecture, candles, statues, paintings of the saints, figures of Mary and Jesus. A group of visiting nuns sang a hymn a cappella. Spontaneously. It took my breath away. Two feelings at once. I was going deeply into my own soul and at the same time I was soaring, joining with the souls of others.

That's the power of spirit. It fuses place, music, art, souls. It gives the everyday world rapture and mystery.

Another memory. Some friends once invited me to their son's bris. As the ceremony began, the father sat holding his son. His father stood behind him. Afterward I saw tears welling up in the grandfather's eyes. He told me that standing behind his son and grandson, he felt the presence of his own father and grandfather. The eternal human chain. Right there. I felt cheated. No one did much to mark special moments in my life. We went through the motions, but the spirit wasn't there.

Do you want your employees to feel the same way you did as a boy?

I never made the connection before. We don't celebrate enough. We're cheating ourselves.

Do you tell stories?

What kind of stories?

Take this conversation. I asked you about spiritual bonds. You told stories. The Emerald Buddha. Your visit to Notre-Dame. Memories of a bris.

A light bulb flashed.

When you first talked to me about spirit and heart, I had no idea what you were talking about. You told stories. Parables. The stream that wanted to cross the desert. The young man too focused on his path to see anything else.

Stories take us to other worlds. They transport us to the world of spirit.

That's hard to buy if you grew up worshiping at the altar of facts and logic.

We're all flooded with facts and detail. More than we can handle. The information tide keeps rising, and the world seems more out of control. Turn on the evening news. What do you see?

He frowned. Murders. Political gridlock. Violence somewhere halfway round the world. It's depressing.

Then you visit Notre-Dame, she said softly. Or you attend a bris. You feel clearer about what you're here to do and why it all makes sense.

Spring flowers were everywhere as he walked to his car. Maybe it's there in the flowers, he thought. He remembered a Zen story. The Buddha preached a sermon by lifting up a flower. The meaning in the flowers is that they're there, he thought. And my meaning is that I'm here. I'm alive.

On the drive home, he was flooded with questions about how to infuse his organization with significance. He laughed. He remembered how often the possessive pronoun *my* had got him in trouble in the past. For people to feel significant, he knew the organization had to be *ours,* not *mine.*

Community and the Cycle of Giving

Find the real world, give it endlessly away
Grow rich, fling gold to all who ask
Live at the empty heart of Paradox
I'll dance there with you, cheek to cheek

—*Rumi*

Leading is giving. Leadership is an ethic, a gift of oneself to a common cause, a higher calling. It is easy to miss the depth and power of that message. These dialogues are intended to encourage readers to deepen their internal journey in search of the gifts they can offer to others.

The essence of leadership is not giving things or even providing visions. It is offering oneself and one's spirit. Material gifts are not unimportant. We need both bread and roses. Soul and spirit are no substitute for wages and working conditions. But what we have all heard is true—the most important thing about a gift is the spirit behind it. When Steve approached gift giving as a material transaction, he failed. When he offered himself, he set in motion a reciprocal process—others gave of themselves in return. The gifts of authorship, love, power, and significance work only when they are freely given and freely received. Leaders cannot give what they do not have or lead to places they've never been. When they try, they breed disappointment and cynicism. When their gifts are genuine and the spirit is right, their giving transforms an organization from a mere place of work to a shared way of life.

The challenge for leaders is to embark on "a journey to find the treasure of your true self, and then [to return] home to give your gift to help transform the kingdom—and in the process your own life. The quest itself is replete with dangers and pitfalls, but it offers great rewards: the capacity to be successful in the world, knowledge of the mysteries of the human soul, the opportunity to find your unique gifts in the world, and to live in loving community with other people."[1]

Authorship, love, power, and significance are not the only gifts that leaders offer. As Maria tells Steve, leaders must learn for themselves the contribution that is theirs to make. Any gifts will work so long as they contribute to the fundamental ethics of compassion and justice. Fused with soul and spirit, gifts form the cornerstones of a purposeful and passionate community.

The Gift of Love

And what is it to work with love?

It is to weave the cloth with threads drawn from your own heart, even as if your beloved were to wear that cloth.

It is to build a house with affection, even as if your beloved were to dwell in that house.

Work is love made visible.

And if you cannot work with love but only with distaste, it is better that you should leave your work and sit at the gate of the temple and take alms of those who work with joy.[2]

When Debashis Chatterjee asked Mother Teresa the secret of her leadership, her answer was simple but profound: "Small work with great love."[3] Love is the true hallmark of great leaders—love for their work and love for those with whom they work. Pressures of the task and the bottom line often crowd out the personal needs that people bring into the workplace. There's always so much to be done. Who has time for kind words or listening or caring? When Robert Galvin (then CEO of Motorola), was asked by his son, Chris (now CEO of Motorola), for his philosophy of business he replied: "Five words: to love and to achieve. And the second will never happen until you do the first." To this day the word *love* is no stranger to people who work at Motorola. Unfortunately, too many modern organizations encourage amiable superficiality and discourage deeper forms of human contact. In most workplaces, the unwritten rules are clear: stay on task, be friendly and upbeat, and avoid anything that hints at emotion or intimacy.

Every organization is a family, whether caring or dysfunctional. Caring begins with knowing—it requires listening, understanding, and accepting. It progresses through a deepening sense of appreciation, respect, and ultimately, love. Love is a willingness to reach out. Steve hesitated to embrace love because he recognized the risk of vulnerability in opening his heart. Embracing that risk lets us drop our masks, meet heart to heart, and be present for one another. We experience a sense of unity and delight in those voluntary, human exchanges that mold "the soul of community."[4]

Love has probably received more attention than any other human emotion. It has many meanings. Plato called it divine madness.[5] The poet Guiraut de Borneil saw a more tender side:

> Love is born, who its fair hope
> Goes comforting her friends.
> For as all true lovers know, love is perfect kindness
> Which is born—there is no doubt—from the heart
> and eyes.
> The eyes make it blossom; the heart matures it
> Love, which is the fruit of their very seed.[6]

Love is largely absent in the modern corporation. Most managers would never use the word in any context more profound than their feelings about food, films, or games. They shy away from love's deeper meanings, fearing both its power and its risks. So it was with Steve. In Topeka, he tried to minimize his risk and liability. Only by accepting anguish and vulnerability—the close companions of love—could he offer a gift that was both accepted and appreciated.

The Gift of Authorship

Authorship is rare in most organizations. Though it may sound like a caricature, the old management approach was pretty simple. Give people jobs. Tell them how to do those jobs. Look over their shoulders to make sure they do the jobs right. Reward or punish them depending on their performance. It was frustrating for everyone. Workers felt overcontrolled, underinformed, and undervalued. Even when they knew how to do the job better than their boss, they felt compelled to follow orders at the expense of performance. Disappointed superiors blamed workers and tightened supervision. A constricting spiral undermined workers' sense of connection, ownership, and pride. So it was, for example, in the old world of General Motors. And it showed in the quality of cars the company produced.

Despite efforts across corporate America to increase participation and enhance the quality of work, tens of thousands of people still see their work as just a job—they put in time, go through the motions, and collect a check. In so doing, they are deprived of the virtues Matthew Fox ascribes to work as distinct from a job: "Work comes from the inside out; work is an expression of our soul, our inner being. It is unique to the individual; it is creative. Work is an expression of the Spirit at work through us."[7]

Around the world, employees assigned to jobs without real work have developed similar levels of cynicism. In the Soviet era, Russian workers elegantly captured the sentiment in the aphorism, "We pretend to work and they pretend to pay us." A similar cynicism has developed among some African American adolescents. Seeing the gates of opportunity largely closed and viewing academic achievement as "acting white," they reject peers who do well in school. Though rejection of institutional norms enables people to stay sane in a world that makes little sense, the price is high. They lose hope of creating a service or product that carries their personal signature. They are cut off from using their talents to contribute something of value to the world.

Giving authorship provides space within boundaries. In an orchestra, the musicians develop their individual parts within the parameters of a particular musical score and the interpretative challenges posed by the conductor. Authorship turns the organizational pyramid on its side. Leaders increase their influence and build more productive organizations. Workers experience the satisfactions of creativity, craftsmanship, and a job well done. Gone is the traditional adversarial relationship in which superiors try to increase their control while subordinates resist them at every turn. Trusting people to solve problems generates higher levels of motivation and better solutions. The leader's responsibility is to create conditions that promote authorship. Individuals need to see their work as meaningful and worthwhile, to feel personally accountable for the consequences of their efforts, and to get feedback that lets them know the results.[8]

Saturn Motors is a tangible showcase of what the gift of authorship can accomplish. GM took some of its employees and gave them a chance to make their own decisions and put their signature on a car someone eventually would drive. As one Saturn employee remarked, "Given the opportunity anyone would like to produce a perfect product. At Saturn they have given us that opportunity, that chance." The ingenuity of employees shows up in the quality of Saturn automobiles, and the loyalty of their customers. Under a plant manager who had given the gift of authorship, one autoworker commented, "We make decisions now. Before, we never made no decisions. We just ran the machine and that was it!"[9]

The Gift of Power

The idea of power as a gift may seem paradoxical. Can anyone ever give power to someone else? Would they even if they could? Realists and revolutionaries have long believed that no one but a fool ever gives power away. Power, they argue, must be seized— forced from the hands of those who hold it. This might be true if giving power always meant becoming weaker. Yet Steve's most important learning at the Topeka plant was that he could give power and wind up stronger.

The gift Steve offered to the worker with the "half-baked idea" was not like a coin placed in an outstretched hand or a neatly wrapped gift placed under a tree. What Steve offered was an *opportunity* for the worker to empower himself. Like all the other gifts that Maria highlighted, the gift of power can be given only to those who want it and are ready to receive it.

Hoarding power produces a powerless organization. People stripped of power look for ways to fight back: sabotage, passive resistance, withdrawal, or angry militancy. Powerlessness fuels rebellion, coercion, even terrorism. We see tragic examples of this self-sealing spiral every day in organizations and societies around the world. Conversely, giving power liberates energy for more productive use. When people have a sense of efficacy and an ability to influence their world, they usually seek to be productive. They direct their energy and intelligence toward making a contribution rather than obstructing progress or destroying their enemies. At Saturn, for example, employees have the power to stop the assembly line when they spot something amiss. A rope with a handle is located at various places along the manufacturing process. Even minor deviation from the company's high standards motivates employees to "pull the rope and stop the line." Giving employees clout has produced a superior product.

The gift of power enrolls people in working toward a common cause. It also creates difficult choice points, like the one Steve faced when an employee "threw a half-baked idea into the hopper." In such circumstances, if leaders say no and clutch power tightly, they reactivate old patterns of antagonism. If they cave in and say yes to anything, they put the organizational mission at risk. Leaders cannot empower others by disempowering themselves. They need to help others find and make productive use of many sources of power—information, resources, allies, access, and autonomy.[10] The workers and managers who banded together at the Topeka plant tapped many of those sources to give their recommendations the power that made it so easy for Steve to say yes.

The gift of power is closely linked to conflict. When power is hoarded and centralized, conflict is often suppressed. Eventually it emerges in coercive or explosive forms. Violence in schools and neighborhoods provides a contemporary example. Feeling powerless, seeing society as an enemy, young people try to empower themselves through gangs and guns. People who feel genuinely powerful will find more productive options. When a highly centralized system begins to loosen up, the initial outcomes are often surprising and disturbing. Previously hidden conflicts leap to the surface. Interest groups battle for scarce resources. This happened all over Eastern Europe after the collapse of Soviet Communism. Effective leadership gives power without undermining the system's integrity. At its best the gift of power makes it possible to confront conflict without warfare and violence. Scott Peck has observed that community is "a place where conflict can be resolved without physical or emotional bloodshed and with wisdom as well as grace."[11]

Authorship and power are related, so the two are easily confused. Space and freedom are at issue in both. Yet there is an important difference. Authorship requires autonomy. Power is the ability to influence others. Artists, authors, scientists, and skilled craftspeople can experience high levels of authorship even when they work largely by themselves. Power, in contrast, is meaningful only in relationship to others. It is the capacity to influence and to get things to happen on a broad scale. Authorship without power is isolating and splintering. Power without authorship can be dysfunctional and oppressive. Each of these two gifts is incomplete. Together, their impact on organizational spirit is extraordinary, a lesson many pioneering companies are beginning to realize.

The Gift of Significance

Several years ago, Continental Airlines was one of the country's poorest-performing airlines. On nearly every measure of performance, the company ranked at the bottom—in number of bags lost, delayed flights, and customer complaints. Enter a new leader, Gordon Bethune. He articulated some clear values: on-time performance, good service, clean airplanes, and convenient destinations. His primary objective was to give employees a coherent sense of meaning and significance. He recognized that significance has both internal and external facets. The internal dimension is the feeling of unity and cohesiveness that goes with being part of a tightly knit community. The external dimension is the sense of pride associated with contributing something of value to the larger society. Continental transformed itself into one of America's top-ranked airlines and even won the distinction of being named the Airline of the Year.

There are potential shadows to tightly knit normative communities. History gives many examples of supposedly liberating societies that turned out to be oppressive, intolerant, or unjust. Every major religion has seen instances of religious leaders who used spiritual authority for selfish or destructive ends. Parallel risks exist in any group or organization. Community, like love, carries risks of dependence, exploitation, and loss. Yet it makes no more sense to reject the ideal of community than to shun intimacy. We need to approach both with a combination of hope and wisdom.

The expressive and symbolic dimensions of experience take many forms: rituals, ceremonies, icons, music, and stories. Humans have always created and used symbols as a foundation for meaning. Organizations without a rich symbolic life become empty and sterile. Going to work is as satisfying as going to a restaurant and eating the menu. What is missed is the joy of eating food and sharing a meal with others. The magic of special occasions is vital in building significance into collective life. Moments of ecstasy are parentheses that mark life's major passages. Without ritual and ceremony, transitions remain incomplete, a clutter of comings and goings. "Life becomes an endless set of Wednesdays."[12]

When ritual and ceremony are authentic and attuned, they fire the imagination, evoke insight, and touch the heart. Ceremony weaves past, present, and future into life's ongoing tapestry. Ritual helps us to face and comprehend life's everyday shocks, triumphs, and mysteries. Both help us experience the unseen webs of significance that tie a community together. When inauthentic, such occasions become meaningless, repetitious, and alienating.

They waste our time, disconnect us from work, and splinter us from one another. "Community must become more than just gathering the troops, telling the stories, and remembering things past. Community must also be rooted in values that do not fail, values that go beyond the self-aggrandizement of human leaders."[13]

Ceremony and ritual may seem extraordinary and exotic, far removed from the ordinary requirements of life. But just as there are grand ceremonies for special occasions, there are simple rituals that infuse meaning, passion, and purpose into daily routine. Both speak to the soul: "A piece of clothing may be useful, but it may also have special meaning to a theme of the soul. It is worth going to a little trouble to make a dinner a ritual by attending to the symbolic suggestiveness of the food and the way it is presented and eaten. Without this added dimension, which requires some thought, it may seem that life goes on smoothly, but slowly soul is weakened and can make its presence known only in symptoms."[14]

Like ritual and ceremony, narrative is a vessel for soul and spirit. It would have been difficult for Steve or Maria to talk about significance without sharing stories. Stories transport us to the magical realm of spirit.

Like night dreams, stories often use symbolic language, therefore bypassing the ego and persona and traveling straight to the spirit and soul, who listen for the ancient and universal instructions embedded there. Because of this process, stories can teach, correct errors, lighten the heart and the darkness, provide psychic shelter, assist transformation and heal wounds. . . . The tales people tell one another weave a strong fabric that can warm the coldest emotional or spiritual nights. So the stories that rise up out of the group become, over time, both extremely personal and quite eternal, for they take on a life of their own when told over and over again.[15]

In successful organizations, people's sense of significance is rooted in shared stories, passed from person to person and generation to generation. These stories are about people, events, triumphs, and tragedies. They transcend time and place. Steve is beginning to understand stories as the symbolic narrative that holds a group together: "Some say that community is based on blood ties, sometimes dictated by choice, sometimes by necessity. And while this is quite true, the immeasurably stronger gravitational field that holds a group together is their stories . . . the common and simple ones they share with one another."[16]

The word *significance* carries dual connotations of meaning and importance. The gift of significance lets people find meaning in work, faith in themselves, confidence in the value of their lives, and hope for the future. Work becomes more joy than drudgery, an opportunity to make a difference as well as a living. Reason and technology often divert our attention from the everyday existential pillars that support our sense of significance. If we lose our gift of fantasy and festival, we lose one of life's most precious pleasures. Steve is now realizing all this for himself.

Sharing

CHAPTER 12

Summoning the Magic of Stories

He wanted to deny it. He no longer could. She was ill. Too many canceled meetings. Delays in returning calls. Weariness in her voice when she finally did. He was praying with new urgency. Prayer might not improve her health, but it was his heartsong, his way of keeping faith. He'd learned it from her. He hoped she could hear it too.

His eyes rebelled against the harsh sunlight. Heat shimmered from the road ahead. Even with the air-conditioning on full blast, it still felt oppressive. It'll be better in the mountains, he thought. A flood of memories was a welcome distraction. He recalled his first trip up this road. How miserable he felt then. She'd helped him find a way out of his private hell. Now he understood that spirit is the real life flow. In his life. In his work. Did she know how much she had given? He hoped so.

A note on her door directed him to the back porch. She was napping there. He'd never seen her asleep. He missed seeing her eyes. They were so important to him. Intense. Beacons on his journey. Reflections of his soul.

He sat and waited. Not for long. She seemed to sense his presence. She smiled broadly when she saw him. Her usual vitality seemed to return.

Steve, I'm glad you're here. There's lemonade in the refrigerator. Get some glasses and plenty of ice. We need something to cope with the heat.

Compared to the city, it's cool. How's Gwen?

Fantastic! She sends her love. The wedding was beautiful. I felt your spirit throughout.

You know how much it meant to us for you to be there. Gwen loved the poem you read.

'In the sea of love I melt like salt.' I'm glad she liked it.

The other thing that's amazing is that the high I've been on since the wedding is carrying over into work.

You can't compartmentalize spirit.

You remember hearing me talk about Jill Stockton?

Maria frowned momentarily. I think so. She's your financial VP, right?

That's her. Floored me a couple of months ago. Came in with an idea for our next management retreat. Said we should tell stories.

Maria smiled. You were surprised?

Totally. She's good. Brilliant, really. Mostly a number cruncher, though. Funny to hear her suggest we swap stories about the year's highs and lows.

Were you pleased?

Beaming! The best thing is, it's not just her. Things like this are taking off all over the place. Team spirit like I'd always hoped for.

What happened with Jill's idea?

A bunch of people got behind it. They made it the centerpiece for our management retreat. We went to this lakeside resort. Beautiful spot. Friday night was the big climax. They'd printed up a fancy program. Billed it as the First Annual Lakeside Lore Hour. All the rules were spelled out in the program.

Rules for what?

For the tournament of tales. Everyone had to share a story at the dinner table. About a peak or a valley from the past year. Then each table had to select its best for the finals.

Nominees to compete for the big prize?

Right. In front of the whole group. Even had an applause meter to pick the winner.

Who won?

Would you believe the plant manager in Topeka?

With a story about you, I'll bet.

You remember my side of the story. I thought I'd pulled off one of the great triumphs in modern corporate leadership. His version was different. He billed it as the real story behind the story.

How embarrassed were you?

Totally. As he tells it, I wasn't leading them. They were leading me. They had the whole thing scripted beforehand. They felt sorry for me after I got so beat up. They figured I'd blow it unless I got a lot of help. After I left, they had a party. A big celebration of their victory over the boss. Even gave me an award, except I wasn't there to accept it.

What was the award?

How to Lead Without Really Trying.

Even secondhand, the story had life. They were both laughing. It felt good.

A great story, she said.

Everyone thought so. People were falling out of their chairs laughing. The applause pushed the meter off the scale.

How were you feeling?

My stomach was in knots. My jaw was clamped so tight it was pretty hard to smile convincingly.

Did you get to respond?

Required by the rules. I was tempted to set the record straight. But I exhaled, took a deep breath, and decided to go with the flow. I kept it short. Roasting the boss is probably good for the soul anyway. I told them that the stories we shared, even one as outlandish as the winner, were the best gift we could give each other. Together we summoned a common spirit.

How'd they react?

Standing ovation. Not just for me. For everyone there. For our community.

I'm proud of you.

I hoped you would be. You made it possible.

I'm only the midwife. You did most of the work. And you felt most of the pain along the way.

The sun had begun its descent toward a gap in the mountains. A faint breeze began to stir. They looked at each other. He felt a deep connection, a tenderness he had rarely felt.

He spoke first. His mouth felt dry. A feeling of anguish was growing in his heart. The words were hard to say.

Pain is what I'm feeling now.

So am I.

Their eyes met, bridging the silence. He knew what they needed to talk about. Would she volunteer? Should he ask? He didn't have to wait long for her response.

You know I haven't been well.

For a long time, he replied. Did he mean it as a rebuke? He wasn't sure. He'd felt she was avoiding the subject. It bothered him.

Do you wonder why I didn't tell you before?

Friends talk to friends. If you really believe in giving, why withhold? He sounded harsher than he intended. He saw the flicker of pain in her face and started to rebuke himself.

Her eyes, as bright and intense as ever, never left his. I haven't talked about my health because I hate being a burden on someone I care about. It's easier for me to offer help than take it from others. One of my cardinal imperfections. Anyway, I'm running out of time. You're very important to me. I think of you as a very special legacy.

His anger and guilt had both evaporated. Pushed aside by an overwhelming sense of gratitude and love. That's a big responsibility, he said.

If it's just another burden, don't take it.

Not a burden. A gift.

Then enjoy giving it away.

CHAPTER 13

Lifting Our Voices in Song

January. Snow flurries outside his office window. A tough day ahead. Lots of balls in the air. The phone rang. He picked it up.

Is this a good time to talk? she asked.

Perfect, he lied. Thanks for returning my call.

I got your message on the machine. You sounded troubled. What's up? she asked.

A classic blooper. It's not easy to screw up the annual holiday party, he said, But somehow we managed.

That's easier than you think. It's certainly not the first time something that was supposed to be special blew up in someone's face. What happened?

You remember the Lakeside Lore tournament?

How could I forget?

Everyone said it was our best meeting ever. Wonderful feeling of community. Only one problem. It was only senior management. We all felt that we wanted a wider audience so we could share the spirit with the rest of the staff.

It's a great idea. The problem is pulling it off with the same spirit. Execution is tricky.

We found that out. A group started meeting after the retreat. Called themselves the Lakesiders. They got excited about doing a music video.

Why a music video?

Something to present at our annual holiday fest. You've talked about music as a way to express spirit. We produced a musical— *The Holiday Spirit: Our Way of Life.*

As a special gift for the holidays?

Seemed like a great idea at the time. Everyone at headquarters came to the party. All the staff. Friends and relatives. You can't believe how much work people put into the production. Making costumes. Rehearsing nights and weekends. Renting musicians from the local symphony.

You put a lot into it. How'd it turn out?

Artistically, the tape was fantastic. I thought everyone would love it. Not true. It flopped.

Do you know why?

Good question. I was stunned. I introduced the tape myself. Gave it a big buildup. After that it was downhill. No enthusiasm. Embarrassing silence. No laughs at the gag lines. Polite applause at the end. My heart was in my throat.

It sounds awfully painful.

Excruciating. As the video was winding down I said a quick prayer for guidance.

Was your prayer answered?

Got help from somewhere. I was at the podium. Scared to death. Trying to figure out what I was going to say to Kurt.

Who's Kurt?

The chief bean counter at corporate. He'd got wind of the musical. He called to tell me it was a dumb way to spend the company's money. I said, 'Don't worry, we'll get a big return.' He wasn't buying. It's hard to talk spirit to Kurt. He's the kind of guy who'd ask for numbers on the salvation rate before he'd join a church.

Once upon a time I had the same feeling about you. Don't write Kurt off too quickly.

Even at my worst I wasn't as much a penny-pinching control freak as Kurt.

She said nothing. He couldn't actually see her raise her eyebrows and roll her eyes over the phone line. But he sensed it.

OK. I'll give Kurt the benefit of the doubt.

So continue the story. You're at the podium and the audience is dying on you. Then what?

I started off by thanking everyone who'd worked on the video. Then I asked the audience: 'Have you ever watched someone open a gift that you gave them? Then seen them try to hide their disappointment?'

That's a nice analogy.

Seemed to work. I told them you always take a risk when you offer a gift. When it's right, it's glorious. But even if it's not, the same spirit is behind it. That spirit is what our organization is about.

You're getting pretty good at thinking on your feet.

Maybe I'm a little better at being myself. And speaking from my heart.

Do you know why the video was the wrong gift?

Sort of. I'm still wrestling with that.

Start with the history. How long has this holiday event been going on?

Years. Way before my time. Same format every year. A lot of people thought it needed a little freshening up.

What was the traditional program?

Open bar. Buffet dinner. And a talent show. Sopranos. Barbershop quartets. Harmonicas. Magicians. Employee amateur hour. No talent required. Always felt like it went on forever.

What happened to the amateur hour this year?

Gone. Replaced by the video.

And you're still wondering why the tape flopped?

He hoped he didn't sound as sheepish as he felt. I guess it's not much of a mystery. We shredded a time-honored ceremony. Should have seen it coming.

Why didn't you?

Hubris, I guess. Maybe we got caught up in the moment. The Lakesiders thought we needed something new. The old format was getting tired. People complained all the time.

Did everyone complain? Who did you hear from?

The Lakesiders mostly. Big mistake in retrospect. Maybe I only heard from the folks who'd already signed on for the new order of service. Most of the audience still liked the old one.

That's an important lesson.

Expensive too. Silence on the line. Enough of my woes. How are you?

Physically, not so great. Spiritually, excited. Do you know Rumi called death our wedding with eternity?

No, I never heard that. He felt a chill. Maria's death was still hard to face.

And I'm making great progress on my book.

What book?

I've given it a tentative title, *Spirited Leadership*. You'll enjoy it. You're in it.

In the chapter on what not to do?

No. You're featured in the chapter on spiritual development. I just hope I have time to get the book done before—

That's a good incentive to hang around. I have plans for you. Big event coming up in April. I really hope you can come.

What's the occasion?

We're celebrating the company's twenty-fifth anniversary.

I'd love to come. It would be a great honor. But I can't promise anything.

It was not what he wanted to hear. After saying good-bye, he sat in silence for several minutes, watching the snow fall outside his window. He thought back to the time he had driven through a blizzard to get to her house. He'd do it again in a moment. Would she make it to April? He took time out for a prayer.

CHAPTER 14

Celebrating Shared Icons

He was midway through his second cup of coffee. Still basking in memories of the night before. The phone rang. It was Maria. She spoke softly. Her voice weak, raspy.

I'm sorry I missed the anniversary celebration. How was it?

Perfect, except for one thing. You weren't there.

I wanted to be. I just couldn't. Fill me in now.

Well, the Lakesiders kept meeting. They put the plan together.

The holiday party disaster didn't faze them?

Spurred them on. They were determined to get it right the next time. Involved everyone they could. Set up a bunch of task forces. Amazing what they got done in a couple of months.

Faith moves mountains. Her voice wavered but her conviction came through as clearly as ever.

We had some big ones to move. A lot of balls in the air. Time crunch. It's tough linking people on four continents. Kurt was on my neck again about wasting money.

Kurt still has faith in the bottom line.

It's his job.

But it all came together?

Barely. The day before launch, it looked pretty dicey.

It always does.

The plan was simple. Honor the past. Celebrate the present. Look toward the future.

Simple but elegant. You covered all the bases.

The history group put together an incredible videotape. With a perfect theme: *From One Seed, Many Plants*. It opened with John Harding doing a rap song.

John? That's hard to imagine. I've known him since he started the company. He's a wonderful man. But he's a little stiff for rapping. My voice is pretty much gone, but, even so, I might still sing better than John.

He could hear her laughing at the other end. He felt better.

John wasn't too crazy about the costume, either. Plaid shirt. Overalls. Pitchfork. Like *American Gothic*. You should have heard him, though, in his best scratchy off-tune baritone. He sounded a little like a German Shepherd growling at the audience. But he put his heart into it—'It was back in Cincinnati that we planted the seed. Tried to build a company I'd be proud to lead.'

Unbelievable. It's totally out of character for John. She was laughing even harder. You have to send me a copy of the tape. It should be the best therapy I've had in a long time.

John loved doing it. A vintage performance. Rave reviews.

That's wonderful. He rarely gets that kind of recognition since he retired.

I owe a lot to John. Without his prodding I'd never have come to see you.

It's a mutual debt. Anyway, what came next?

After John's verse, the camera shifts to the chorus behind him. Out steps the original Topeka plant manager to pick up the lyrics. And it went on like that. Our history. Played out right in front of us. Every era and every site. Very moving.

I can't wait to see it.

The audience was mesmerized. They'd all heard of John. A company legend. But a lot of them had never seen him. Old-timers savored the memories. Newcomers devoured the stories. Everyone loved it.

They usually do. At least when you get the right themes.

Unlike our holiday video. So then it was on to the present. We did this round-the-world televised tour of our facilities. People, places, products. All live with a satellite hookup. The price tag on that one was a tough sell with Kurt. It was worth it. Even he said so later. First time we could all be at the same party. See each other. Talk to each other. Celebrate together. A big family reunion.

John must have been proud.

It's the first time I ever saw him in tears.

Knowing John, that's remarkable.

He wasn't alone. The feelings were so intense. I was just hoping we could make it through the last part.

The future.

Right. We opened with another video. Young people from around the world. Employees and customers. Talking about their dreams—what they hoped we'd become. Powerful, eloquent, inspired stuff. Reminded me how crazy it was when I thought I was supposed to be the sole source of vision.

You've learned a lot since then. You've developed the courage to let others lead.

I needed more courage than that. I was supposed to close off the event.

The video must have been a tough act to follow.

I was too choked up to give my prepared speech. It wouldn't have worked anyway. The young people on the tape had said it all.

What did you do?

I talked about you.

You talked about me?

You. I was bone honest. I told them the truth. When I first came into this job, I wasn't ready. I didn't know it at the time, but John did. I told them he put me in touch with a wonderful woman. My spiritual guide. She taught me that leading is giving. That spirit is the core of life. Helped me find my soul. Then I said to the audience: 'All of you have been my teachers as well. Together, we're finding the company's soul. We're building an uncommon spirit. One seed, many plants, a shared dream.'

Silence on the other end of the line. He knew she was crying. So was he.

Thank you, Steve. Thank you very much. It means a lot to me. Be sure to send me the tape.

Expressing the Spirit

The most beautiful and profound emotion we can experience is the sensation of the mystical. It is the sower of all true science. He to whom this emotion is a stranger, who can no longer wonder and stand rapt in awe, is as good as dead. To know that what is impenetrable to us really exists, manifesting itself as the highest wisdom and the most radiant beauty, which our dull faculties can comprehend only in their primitive forms—this knowledge, this feeling, is at the center of true religion.

—*Albert Einstein*

We go to services and read prescribed words, not to find God but to find a congregation, to find other people who are in search of the same divine presence as we are. By coming together, singing together, reading the same words together, we overcome the isolation and solitude with which each of us ordinarily lives. We all become one and we create the moment in which God is present.

—*Rabbi Harold Kushner*

The Limits of Rationality

Modern managers concentrate mostly on the rational side of enterprise. Neglecting the spiritual dimension of work, they overlook a powerful untapped source of energy and vitality. The costs of this omission are obscured by deep devotion to the myth that reason can solve all problems. In *The Feast of Fools*, Harvey Cox calculates the costs: "Man in his very essence is *homo festivus* and *homo fantasia*. Celebrating and imagining are integral parts of his humanity but western industrial man in the past few centuries has begun to lose his capacity for festivity and fantasy."[1] Cox adds that the loss is personal, social, and religious. It deprives us of a central ingredient of our lives. It makes us provincial and maladaptive. It stills our sense of connection to the cosmos, of contributing to something larger than ourselves.

Steve has felt these costs firsthand. They were at the root of his discouragement when he first visited Maria. His life had become flat, dull, and lacking in contour. Devoted to the church of hard work and reason, he paid no attention to his own or his organization's spiritual core. To summon spirit, Steve learns to embrace the symbolic discourse of spirit: art, ritual, stories, music, and icons.

Expressive activity is integral to meaningful human enterprise. Its absence kills faith and hope. People put in time without passion or purpose. Though fictional, the events in the dialogues between Steve and Maria are based on direct observations made in many successful organizations. Viewed from the outside, the pink Cadillacs, diamonds, and other symbols of Mary Kay Cosmetics, for example, may appear superficial and hokey. For insiders, symbols and ceremonies help to anchor the organization's soul and release its spirit.

Even newcomers and outsiders can savor the spirit of a good ceremony. A mechanical engineer went to pick up his new automobile, a Saturn. He arrived to find it sitting in front of the showroom. As he was handed his keys, all the employees—mechanics, clerks, accountants, custodians—gathered around and sang to him. He said later that he thought he was simply buying a car, but now felt as if he had joined a family.

Story as Public Dream

Early in his dialogues with Maria, Steve discovered the magic of stories. Throughout history, people have relied on narrative to express spiritual messages hard to communicate any other way. Successful organizations are storied organizations. One does not have to be there long or go very far to learn the lore. Many contemporary organizations regularly convene times for storytelling.

Over time, layers of story accumulate to help people touch the dream world of corporate mythology. Without story and myth, there is no public dream. Without shared dreams, organizations falter and perish. "A dream is a personal experience of that deep, dark ground that is the support of our conscious lives, and a myth is the society's dream. The myth is the public dream and the dream is the private myth."[2]

Individuals, groups, and organizations all need their own stories. As B. Lopez observes: "Remember only this one thing, the stories people tell have a way of taking care of them. If stories come to you care for them. And learn to give them away when they are needed. Sometimes a person needs a story—more than food to stay alive. That is why we put these stories in each others' memories. This is how people care for themselves." Leaders must venture off the known and protected pathway to find their own private storehouse. Those stories help them choose a direction and learn from their experiences. "We tell stories to illuminate the paths we travel, and to share humor, courage and wisdom in this liberation struggle."[3]

Maria's stories provided a temporary beacon on Steve's path to spiritual liberation until he began to spin tales of his own. He was then able to help his company along its own spiritual path. The winning story at the lakeside retreat will take its place in the evolving legend. The moral: leaders need followers. The real drive comes from below.

Music as Enhancement

Steve's venture into music as a way to summon spirit provides an important warning. Expressive activity is powerful. When it works, it is majestic. When it goes awry, it can backfire resonantly, leaving in its wake suspicion, feelings of manipulation, and a sense of betrayal. The composers of the ill-fated musical had a good idea. Their effort misfired because they lost sight of tradition and misread their audience. The resulting performance evoked disappointment and alienation instead of building spirit.

Susanne Langer observes that "music is the algebra of feelings."[4] A movie without music is like food without spice or a summer morning without birds singing in the trees. Music is a language of spirit: "Words tend to destroy the magic, to desecrate the feelings, and to break the most delicate fabrics of the soul which have taken this form just because they were incapable of formulation in words, images, or ideas."[5]

Music inspired Steve's epiphany at Notre-Dame. The a cappella singing was as essential as the majesty of the setting in creating a powerful spiritual experience. The same power of music is essential in modern organizations. Thomas Watson Sr., who built International Business Machines into one of the most successful companies in the world, understood the importance of singing. IBM used to publish a company song book so that IBMers could sing together. Watson and the songbook have long since disappeared, and it's easy to dismiss the idea of a company songbook as a quaint relic. Yet who knows how much loss of heart contributed to IBM's fall from grace in the 1980s?

Walter Durrig, former commander of the Swiss Army, summed it up with a Swiss-German phrase, *singe oder seckla*. Roughly translated, it means "either sing or haul ass."

The Role of History and Icons

Jay Featherstone refers to America as the "United States of Amnesia" because we have so little appreciation of the significance of history. Without roots, plants perish. Without history, the present makes no sense. Without a historical base, a vision is rootless and doomed. As Steve comes to grips with the gift of significance, he realizes the vital role of history in the spiritual life of an organization. In the misguided musical interlude, ignoring history undermined the event. In the twenty-fifth anniversary celebration, the planners learned from their prior mistake. As employees around the world reviewed the history of their organization, they strengthened their sense of shared connection and ownership. His-story became our story. It provided an organic platform for the present and a launching pad for the future.

To summon spirit and care for the soul, we must relearn ancient lessons. There is truth beyond rationality. The bottom line is not the ultimate criterion. There is another dimension. Almost every organization touches this realm from time to time— in retirement parties, holiday gatherings, award banquets, or other special occasions. Too often such events are last-minute occurrences, hastily planned and halfheartedly attended. People see them as they are: mechanical and spiritless, pale reflections of what they could and should be. Disease of the spirit exacts a high price. Spiritual bankruptcy ultimately leads to economic failure. The deeper cost is creating a world in which everything has a function yet nothing has any meaning. Our shrunken psyches are "just as much a victim of industrialization as were the bent bodies of those luckless children who were once confined to English factories from dawn to dusk."[6]

A New Life

CHAPTER 15

The Twilight of Leadership

Her call was a surprise. Never before had she called to request a meeting. At first he didn't recognize her voice. Even more disturbing, he sensed her real purpose. She wanted to say good-bye. He tried to lie to himself. Pretend it was something else. Deep down he knew he had to face the truth.

The familiar road to her house again brought back memories. How nervous he was the first time they met. The time she told him to get lost, and he did. The many times she had turned his questions back to him—keeping his journey alive and on track. He felt nervous again, but for another reason. When they first met, he was desperate about his life. Now he was fearful for hers.

As he pulled up the familiar drive, he hoped to see her standing at the doorway. She wasn't there.

He found her sitting in her favorite chair, cloaked in a colorfully embroidered soft-silk caftan. Her brown eyes seemed even more vivid than he remembered them, her smile as warm and enigmatic as ever. Then he looked more closely. Her eyes seemed more vital only because her face was so pale and thin. There was a hint of sadness that he had never seen before.

I'm so glad you could come, she said softly.

He knew she was making a noble effort to look strong. Her voice gave her away.

You know I can't stay away for long. He tried to sound upbeat.

Thanks for the videotape. What a wonderful event! I talked to John. He called it a spiritual masterpiece, a work of art. He's very proud. So am I.

You made it possible. Without your—

She held up her hand. I didn't ask you here for that. I need to tell you something. I'm running out of time. This is probably it— our last meeting.

He knew it was coming. He still wasn't prepared.

I don't know how long I have, she continued. It isn't much.

I've been trying to convince myself otherwise.

Me too, for as long as I could. Neither of us can deny it anymore. I wanted us to have some time together before I go. You're very important to me. More than you'll ever know. I love gardening because I love seeing growth. There's great joy in nourishing something and helping it along. It's a lot like parenting. Our time together has been a wonderful gift for me.

He made no effort to resist the feelings that surged from somewhere deep inside.

You're the parent I never had. Dad died when I was young. I was close to Mother, but she was a conscience more than a coach. You've been my guide. You're who I want to become.

Her eyes deepened. Do you remember our first meeting? she asked.

Every minute. I thought about it and all the others on the drive up. How scared I was at first. Feeling the bottom dropping out of my life. Nothing made any sense. Nothing I did made things any better.

That happened to me once. A long time ago. Before you were born. Remember how your career was the only thing that mattered? I was the same way. Maybe even more single-minded. It was tough back then, really tough, for a woman. Top jobs went to men. I had to be smarter and work harder. It was the only way to get ahead. I made a lot of sacrifices.

That's why I touched a nerve when I asked about pictures?

Not just a nerve. You touched my soul. She stopped and closed her eyes. I only fell in love once. Not wisely, but too well.

He was married. I got pregnant. I agonized for weeks. My career or my baby?

He had never felt so much empathy for someone else. Nor so much love. His throat tightened. He swallowed hard. He didn't want to cry. He did anyway.

She waited. Then she continued, haltingly. My heart told me to have the baby. My mind said I couldn't keep it. My heart won. He was a boy. Tommy. She stopped and looked down. He could see the tears on her cheeks. He was beautiful. The most wonderful gift I ever received. Then he was gone. SIDS, I guess they'd say now. He's still with me. Every day. He'd be about your age.

Why didn't you tell me? He felt her anguish. He wished he hadn't asked.

She looked down. They sat in silence for several minutes.

At first I didn't make the connection. If I had, I still wouldn't have told you.

Why not?

That wasn't our agreement. You came for spiritual guidance, even if you didn't know it at first. My job was to help you on a journey. Now my journey here is ending. There's more. I want you to know it all. After Tommy's death, I tried to lose myself in my career. A lot like you did. I got a chance to start my own business. I was lucky—in the right place at the right time. The business became my child. I put everything into making it a success. It worked—beyond my wildest dreams.

I've heard the stories. You're a legend.

There are other things you don't know. Almost no one does.

Why did you leave your business? Wasn't that like giving your child away?

I got sick. Real sick. I was in a lot of pain. I didn't want anyone to know. It was crazy—the leader isn't supposed to get ill. I started using painkillers. I got more addicted to the pills than to my work. I took a long holiday in Europe. That was the cover story. The truth was I checked into a clinic near Paris. I was looking for medical help. I found more than that. There was a priest there—a very wise man. I've never met anyone with a more ecumenical sense of human spirit. At first he made about as much sense to me as I did to you in our early meetings. But he was patient, and very persistent.

A lot like you.

I hope so. He helped me find a different path.

Like you helped me.

After Tommy's death, I'd walled off life's deeper questions. The priest showed me that I had to explore them. When I did, I realized they were more real and more important than anything else. He helped me find a new path. I'd already done what

I set out to do in business. My company, my second child, was a success. I'd nurtured my successors. I had enough money. I turned over the business to the next generation. I recreated my life around three passions: art, gardening, and spirit.

And helping others. Being a spiritual parent.

That was my new vocation. Helping people along their spiritual paths.

You've helped me find my soul. Challenged me to lead from my heart. Helped me bring spirit to my company. It's a debt I can never repay.

You've already paid in full—with interest.

They sat face to face for several minutes. They didn't need to speak. The silence spoke eloquently—two souls joined together. Then a sharp pain traveled across her face, breaking the moment.

He knew her store of energy was gone. He wanted to stay. He knew it was time to leave. He walked over and held her hands. He remembered how comforting her touch had once been for him. He hoped his touch felt as comforting to her now. She reached over to the small table nearby. She handed him a small envelope. He recognized her stationery. For later, she said.

Your work will go on, he said, surprised that it came out as a whisper.

I know. I'll be seeing you.

He barely made it
to his car. Biting his
lip, he fumbled for his
keys. A rush of tears pre-
vented him from finding
the ignition. He slumped over
the steering wheel and cried.
Pull yourself together, he

thought. What if she's watching? Then he did the only thing
that made any sense. He took a walk around the lake.

He came to the stream where he and Maria had once watched
a leaf float by. He sat down and opened the envelope. She had
handwritten a short note:

Dear Steve,

More than 400 years ago, the great Italian poet
Dante gave poetic form to the journey of his own soul.
He cast Virgil as his guide through the inferno. At the
end of the journey, Virgil takes his leave. Sometimes it's
hard to say what's in our hearts. Virgil's timeless farewell
says what's in mine for you:

You have seen the fires of passion and hell,
My son, and now you arrive
Where I myself can see no further.
I have brought you here by wit and by art.
You take as your guide your heart's true pleasure.
You have passed through the steep and narrow places
And now the sun shines bright
upon your brow.
See around you the flowers and young grasses
which the soil of paradise grows.
Your eyes, whose weeping once
brought me to you,
now shine far and full of bliss.
I can go no further.
Expect from me no further word or sign
Your feel is right, and sound, and free.
To disobey it would be a fault.
Therefore, I give you yourself
crowned and mitered, you are yours.[1]

    A flush of love and pride played against his deep sadness.

CHAPTER 16

Deep Refuge

The funeral was over. He was alone. He knew that. Still, he felt her there. He found himself talking to her. Was he crazy? Talking to a ghost? He didn't care.

He remembered the Saturday evening she died. He and Gwen were spending a rare night alone. Sitting, talking, and touching. Jazz in the background. The doorbell was a surprise. Intrusive, unwelcome. It was John. His face said it all. Maria was dead.

Steve remembered putting his arms around John. They'd never hugged before. You'd have been proud, he said.

He remembered the awkwardness. Gwen taking charge. Getting them into the living room. Pouring wine. Asking them to talk about Maria. Stories. Tears. Laughter. Tears again.

He was talking to her now. As if she were there.

At first all I could think about was the void. Who would fill it? How could I go on without you? I didn't think I could. Then I realized your spirit is still here, deep in my heart. It always will be, as long as I keep it alive.

I remember going to your house before the memorial service. Everything still there. The garden. The art. In your bedroom, I found a picture of Tommy. You did keep a photo of someone. Maybe it was enough. I wished Tommy could be there. We could have been friends.

He stopped for a while. Sat in silence. It felt strange to be talking with someone who wasn't there. Why? He remembered what he'd learned from her. He talked to her again.

I hope the funeral was what you wanted. Simple. Elegant. From the heart. A reflection of you.

He reviewed in his mind all the stories that her friends had shared. How they came to know her. What she was like. What she had meant to them. Almost everyone there had made their own personal offering. It was John's story that he found himself reviewing and savoring more than any other. He tried to see it all in his mind's eye. A hotel ballroom. A big crowd assembled for a testimonial roast in John's honor. A series of roasters, each more irreverent than the last. Then the MC announcing the evening's featured entertainment—direct from Tokyo, Japan's most revered Kabuki player, Marinari Takehashi. An elegant singer in traditional makeup and full kimono padding gently to center stage. A beautiful voice singing Japanese opera. Marinari bowing deeply and walking over to John. Then, to his complete surprise, jumping in his lap and hugging him enthusiastically. John recoiling in shock. Marinari then whispering in his ear, *Hajimemashite. Gotcha, John-san!* John collapsing in laughter when he finally realized that the great Kabuki singer in his arms was none other than Maria.

The entire service had been a beautiful recollection of an extraordinary person. A unique life that enriched so many others.

He spoke to her again.

Maybe you know how much I struggled over what to say. The right words never seemed to come. I'd bought a book of Rumi's poems because you liked them so much. As I read it, the right verse jumped off the page. It said just what I wanted to say. I hope you heard it.

He recited the poem again, slowly:

> Three companions for you:
> Number one, what you own. He won't even leave
> the house
> for some danger you might be in. He stays inside.
> Number two: your good friend. He at least comes to
> the funeral.
> He stands and talks at the graveside. No further.
> The third companion, what you do, your work,
> goes down into death to be there with you, to help.
> Take deep refuge with that companion, beforehand.[1]

After I finished, I looked at faces in the audience. Through my tears I could see theirs. I knew you were with us.

The Cycle of
the Spirit

Clay lies still, but blood's a rover;
Breath's a ware that will not keep.
Up, lad: when the journey's over
There'll be time enough to sleep.

—A. E. Housman

The spiritual cycle has come full circle. In facing Maria's death, Steve begins to anticipate the twilight of his own spiritual journey. Death brings terror. It also brings new life, and renewed appreciation for life's gifts. When we wed, we leave one family to join a new one. When we die, we let go of this world to rejoin eternity.

Sherwin Nuland reminds us how little we control the timing and the manner of our final exit.[1] When it comes, the end is often messy and painful rather than peaceful and dignified. We know that we will die, but continually seek to push this sobering reality into the shadows of consciousness. Becker writes that "everything man does in his symbolic world is an attempt to deny and overcome his grotesque fate."[2] The question is whether we must see this fate as grotesque. To deny our destiny is to succumb to fear. To accept it, and to recognize that we contribute through our death as through our life is liberating. It opens new possibilities for life and for leadership.

We usually associate leadership with birth and growth. Rarely do we see much promise in twilight or eclipse. Like all of us, leaders often deny their own mortality and pretend that what they have built will last forever.

An old Sufi tale captures this existential burden. It tells of Jesus walking by a flock of sheep and whispering something in the ear of one. Later, the sheep stopped eating and drinking. Several days later, Jesus again passed by the flock and asked the shepherd why the one sheep appeared to be in such poor health. The shepherd, unaware of to whom he was speaking, replied that someone had passed by and whispered something in the sheep's ear. The tale closes with this moral: "If you are curious to know what the venerable Jesus said in the sheep's ear, let me tell you. What the blessed Jesus said was: 'Death exists.' Although it was only an animal, when it heard of death, that sheep stopped eating and went into this state of stupor."[3]

There was a time when Maria's death would have left a gaping wound in Steve's heart and served as a depressing reminder of his own mortality. We all know the power of the grief and loss that follow the death of someone we love. Steve is learning anew that these feelings are inescapable. But his spiritual journey has given him a new perspective on death. Finding his own soul has opened his heart and enabled him to understand that all of us "are continually dying one another's lives and living one another's deaths."[4]

As Steve's personal wounds became the eye to discover his soul, his acceptance of Maria's death is opening new possibilities for his leadership. Sadness and the need to mourn are still with him. But he understands at a deep level that he can best express his love and gratitude by honoring the gifts Maria has given him and offering them in turn to others. He can now begin each day expecting the unexpected, optimistic that he will find among chaos and confusion opportunities to shape an enduring human institution. He can see more clearly how individual efforts can accumulate into a shared historical legacy. "No matter what he does, every person on earth plays a central role in the history of the world. And normally he doesn't know it."[5]

Becker finds purpose and even optimism in embracing rather than denying death as the end of life's spiritual journey: "The most that any of us can seem to do is to fashion something—an object or ourselves—and drop it into the confusion, make an offering of it, so to speak, to the life force."[6]

When we succumb to greed, focus solely on the bottom line, and worship only at the altar of rationality, we undermine our search for meaning, passion, and a sense of life's deeper, spiritual purpose. Steve was fortunate to find a guide who challenged and encouraged him to search for his own heart and soul. That search required him to confront deeply the central questions of meaning and faith: What did he believe? How did he understand the universe and his place in it? He faced the central choice point posited by Andrew Greeley:

It seems to me that in the last analysis there are only two choices: Macbeth's contention that life is a tale told by an idiot, full of sound and fury and signifying nothing, and Pierre Teilhard's "something is afoot in the universe, something that looks like gestation and birth." Either there is plan and purpose—and that plan and purpose can best be expressed by the words "life" and "love"—or we live in a cruel, arbitrary, and deceptive cosmos in which our lives are a brief transition between two oblivions. The data are inconclusive as to these two choices, at least if we look at the data from a rational, scientific standpoint. . . . I opt for hope, not as an irrational choice in the face of the facts, but as a leap of faith in the goodness I have experienced in my life.[7]

As he encountered his soul, Steve made the same decision to opt for hope. He was able to see gifts of leadership as an expression of his confidence in life and love and as a way to help his organization discover a new and vibrant faith. He became, in Kierkegaard's phrase, a "knight of faith":

This figure is the man who lives in faith, who has given over the meaning of his life to his creator, and who lives

centered on the energies of his maker. He accepts whatever happens in this visible dimension without com-
plaint, lives his life as a duty, faces his death without
qualms. No pettiness is so petty that it threatens his
meaning; no task is too frightening to be beyond his
courage. He is fully in the world on its terms and wholly
beyond the world in his trust of the invisible dimension.
The knight of faith then represents what we call an
ordeal of mental health, the continued openness of life
out of the death throes of dread.[8]

Nineteenth-century captains of industry led America's organizations to international preeminence. Captains of industry were
gradually replaced by modern managers who have helped us see
the virtues of clear goals, measurable objectives, specialization,
policy, and accountability. We have come a long way from our
ancestors who worked intimately with nature in families and
small communities. We face challenges today that fall beyond the
reach of both the captains of industry and modern managers.
Technological breakthroughs have created previously unknown
conveniences and efficiencies. Yet we still face an onslaught of
vexing problems that are frustratingly recalcitrant in the face of
our search for rational and technical solutions.

More and more of us have come to see that many of these persistent and troublesome problems are rooted in a disease of the human spirit. Jimmy Carter may have been ahead of his time when he suggested that America was suffering from a spiritual malaise. Few of his fellow citizens thanked him at the time, but Bill Clinton returned to the same theme fifteen years later. It was a popular message, even if Clinton himself turned out to be a deeply flawed role model for spiritual renewal. Nor is this message restricted to Baptists, southerners, or Democrats. Lee Atwater, one of the architects of Ronald Reagan's political success, talked about the "spiritual vacuum in the heart of the American society, this tumor of the soul," and George W. Bush made faith a recurring theme in his presidential campaign. In another niche of American society, the same message was echoed by a self-described "unemployed, impoverished, chronically ill, disabled and usually homeless" man in Nashville. He wrote in the editorial page of the local newspaper, "Our nation is having a severe and major spiritual crisis in which the future of the country is in great danger."

To prevail in the face of violence, homelessness, malaise, and the many other spiritual challenges of modern life, we need a vision of leadership rooted in the enduring sense of human wisdom, spirit, and heart. We need a new generation of seekers—

Marias and Steves who have the courage to confront their own
demons, the strength to embark on a personal quest for spirit
and heart, and the commitment to share their learning with
others.

How will we develop the seekers that we need? To begin with,
we need a revolution in how we think about leadership and how
we develop leaders. Most management and leadership development programs ignore or demean spirit. They desperately need
an infusion of spiritful forms such as poetry, literature, music,
art, theater, history, philosophy, and dance. Even that would leave
us far short of the cadre of leaders of spirit that we require. Leaders learn most from their experience—especially from their fail-
ures. Too often, though, they miss the lessons. They lack the
reflective capacity to learn on their own and have not been fortunate enough to find a spiritual guide, a Maria, who can help
them sort things through to find their own spiritual center.

In recent decades, we have evolved a kind of implicit compact
with the most senior members of our community. In return for
better medical care and more financial independence, they are
expected to go off to play bridge or golf, leaving the rest of us to
get on with our everyday pursuits. The implicit message is that
we want them to be comfortable, even though they are largely
useless. We have thus cordoned off potential sources of spiritual

insight in retirement homes and communities, where their wisdom and experience are rarely available to the less experienced.

Especially in an era that places a premium on speed and technical precocity, leaders like Steve often find themselves confronting awesome challenges with inadequate reservoirs of experience or seasoning. They look to books, articles, consultants, and workshops to find the latest solutions-in-good-standing. When those fail, they turn to the next fad. Yet there are countless potential Marias in the world—sources of spiritual guidance who are untapped or underused. A return to spirituality will lead us to seek their wisdom. In matters of spirit, wisdom and experience count far more than technique or strategy.

Like Maria, great spiritual teachers from many cultures and traditions have believed that wisdom comes from within rather than without. This message is the central point of a story told repeatedly in many different spiritual traditions. The poet and mystic Andrew Harvey offers a Sufi rendition of the tale:

> There was a man who lived in Istanbul, a poor man. One night he dreamed vividly of a very great treasure. In a courtyard, through a door, he saw a pile of blazing jewels heaped by the side of an old man with a beard. In the dream, a voice told him an address, 3 Stassanopoulis

Street, Cairo. Because he had learned enough to trust his dream visions, he went on a long arduous journey to 3 Stassanopoulis Street in Cairo. One day, many years later, he came to that doorway, entered through it into a court-yard full of light, saw the old man from his dream sitting on the bench, went up to him, and said, "I had a dream many years ago, and in the dream I saw you sitting exactly where you are sitting now, and I saw this great heap of treasure by you. I have come to tell you my dream and to claim my treasure." The old man smiled, embraced him, and said, "How strange, I had a dream last night that under a bed in a poor house in Istanbul there was the greatest treasure I have ever seen." At that moment, the poor man saw that what he had been look-ing for all those years was really under his own bed, in his own heart, at the core of his own life.[9]

The responsibility of the guide is not to give answers but to raise questions, suggest directions, and offer support. "Man is reborn, no longer born of the flesh, but reborn of the spirit, of the inspiration from within and the teacher without."[10]

If we look for guidance, no doubt we can find it. There is always the risk of false prophets—charismatic figures like Jim

Jones, David Koresh, or Luc Jouret. We should be profoundly skeptical of anyone who offers a faith built on values of exclusivity, isolation, and intolerance. But there are many teachers whose spirituality is solidly rooted in love, understanding, and justice. Their wisdom and faith may help us reclaim and regain our hearts, our souls, and our spirit. Our journey is a search, often arduous, for our spiritual center. Once we find our own light within, we can share it with others, offering our own gifts from the heart.

CHAPTER 17

The Legacy

A month later, Steve was at his desk, wondering what was on Jill Stockton's mind. It's personal, she'd said, when she asked to meet. His reverie was soon interrupted. Jill was there. With no trace of her usual cheerful smile.

She took a seat. He waited for her to take the lead.

It's your fault, she said. I was fine until you started all this talk about spirit.

And now?

It always seemed pretty straightforward before. I worked hard in college. Did well in business school. My career is going well. I'm a darn good finance officer.

One of the best, he said.

My marriage is great. The kids are doing well. So why am I starting to ask what's life all about?

A wakeup call. From your soul.

What soul? I don't even know what the word means.

That explains the call.

So do I pick up the phone and say, 'Is that you, soul?'

Might work. But you don't really need a phone. You need to look inside yourself.

Meaning what?

Listen to your heart.

She glanced briefly toward the door.

Are you thinking you should break for the exit before I say something even crazier? he asked.

She laughed and relaxed a little. How'd you know?

I've been there.

I'm good with numbers and financials. When you tell me to look inside, listen to my heart, I don't even know where to begin.

How often do you pray?

She stared at him, a look of surprise spreading across her face. He could see it was a question she hadn't expected.

When she spoke, the words came slowly. I don't. Who would I pray to?

Maria taught me that prayer is a heartsong. It's one way to talk to your soul.

And what is my soul supposed to tell me?

Maybe that the only place you can find what you're looking for is in the cave you're afraid to enter.

Jill fell into startled, uncharacteristic silence. Then, as she stared at Steve, her mouth slowly relaxed into a smile. In my dreams it's not actually a cave. It's a dark room. Someone's after me, and that dark room is the only way to escape. But I'm too scared to go in. So I'm trapped.

I've been there. That's what took me to Maria.

You found what you were looking for?

More than once.

So can you give me a preview of what's ahead?

I can't tell you what's in your heart. Only you can do that.

He smiled as he remembered his first meeting with Maria. She'd told him the same thing. To everything a season, he thought, and a time to every purpose. Time now to help someone else on her journey.

Postlude

Continuing a
Spirited Dialogue

In the first edition of *Leading with Soul*, we invited readers to share their experiences in integrating soul into their lives at work and at home. We are grateful to the many who responded and shared accounts from their life journeys. Letters came from all over the world. Responses were rich, moving, and varied. Many readers also posed questions, many of which we had not considered as we wrote the book. Here we share some readers' questions and offer responses drawn from our own experience and from the many stories that readers have shared.

We begin with questions about the book itself: why did we write it, and what were our hopes for it? Then we take on some specific and personal how-to questions. These have often taken the form, "Sure, it sounds good, but how do I actually do it? How can I put any of these ideas into practice?" Finally, we discuss some questions that move beyond personal spirituality to focus on issues of spiritual development in the larger world: what's happening now, and what might happen in the future?

Queries About the Book

Why did you write about spirit and soul?

It was not a book we had planned on writing. It emerged as an unexpected calling during an informal lunch with our publisher, Jossey-Bass. We arrived that day with a list of possible book projects, all well within our social science comfort zone. Partway through the meeting, Lynn Luckow, president of Jossey-Bass at the time, deliberately interrupted the conversation's flow to ask a simple, inspired question: "What do you *really* want to do? Blue-sky it." Silence fell over the breaking of bread and sipping of wine as we both gradually realized the awful truth: we didn't *know* what we *really* wanted to do. Out of that silence came an unexpected reply: "We'd like to do a book about leadership and spirit." (Thanks again, Lynn, for being the godfather of this project.)

That answer put us on an unfamiliar and scary path. We had committed to write a book even though we had only a hazy idea of where we were going and what we had to say. Fortunately, many friends and colleagues came to our rescue with ideas and support. We plunged into the great spiritual literature from around the world: the Bible, the Tao, the Koran, the Bhagavad-Gita, Sufi poetry, Native American mythology, African American folk tales, the Tibetan Book of the Dead, and many other works. All these helped greatly, but they were not enough. We also had to go deep inside to find our own spiritual centers. We couldn't write about anyone else's spiritual journey without examining and deepening our own. We couldn't talk about soul and spirit without experiencing firsthand what they meant for us.

For Terry, this journey triggered a conversation with his wife, Sandy, that eventually led him to give up a tenured position at Vanderbilt University so that he and Sandy could fulfill their dream of returning home to California to design and build a house on the central coast. It also enabled him to revisit a painful chapter in his life that he had neglected for many years—the tragic death in 1964 of his five-year-old son Barry. The impact on Lee was equally profound—difficult but essential reappraisals of a painful divorce and the death of his father, a recommitment to religious faith, and a move to Kansas City and the University of Missouri after more than twenty years at Harvard University.

In the end we wrote the book for others because we hoped to help them in their search for meaning and faith. And we wrote it for ourselves because, even if we didn't know it at the time, it was what we needed to do.

*Did you consciously choose Maria at the outset
as the spiritual guide?*

Maria evolved as we wrote. She began as a nameless, hermitlike he. But our hermit didn't seem to be up to the job—he lacked warmth and heart. Maria gradually took shape, evolving into a fuller person as the story developed. Adam and Eve, Mars and Venus exist in all of us. That helps to explain why we needed the spiritual guide to be a woman, whereas Susan Trott, in her wise and delightful book *The Holy Man,*[1] chooses a male as her title character. Maria made our story work and helped us explore the feminine and the masculine in ourselves.

I liked the book, but did it change me? Was it supposed to?

Some readers tell us that the book changed them profoundly. Others feel let down, waiting for something dramatic but not experiencing it yet. The variety of the individual responses convinces us that the reader, not the book, is the true author of change. Your responses to *Leading with Soul* are clues to understanding where you are on your own spiritual journey.

For some readers, *Leading with Soul* has served as a guide or map for rekindling soul and spirit in relationships. Many individuals report discovering ways to make individual journeys less lonely and shared quests even more fulfilling. More than one couple told us that their joint reading of the book opened a dialogue that strengthened or even saved their marriage.

For other readers the book has confirmed a path they have been on for some time. As a reader from Iowa wrote: "I felt I was on the right track, but it sure felt awfully lonely and scary. With Steve and Maria as my companions, I gained new strength and courage to plow ahead." An art teacher wrote: "An instructor gave me a copy of *Leading with Soul* to read. I have no idea what this book has touched inside of me, but it feels good. As a 27-year-old African American male I feel lost in this society. Your book has challenged me to start where few of us do . . . with our souls."

A number of readers reported giving *Leading with Soul* to colleagues, friends, or loved ones, hoping it might serve others as it had them. Sometimes that gift has been inspired. An undergraduate wrote that his father gave him "a copy of the book to read. Initially, I wasn't really sure why. But after reading the book I figured it out. He wanted me to have the same kind of experience he had. I think it made him a better boss. But I know it's made him a really good dad."

Some individuals encounter the book when they are, like Jill in the final chapter, on the verge of a wakeup call from their soul—when questions of identity, faith, and direction beckon with growing urgency. The letter of one such reader, a Japanese manager, captures in a powerful and poignant way the feelings many others share in today's chaotic and confusing world:

Impressions of *Leading with Soul* Humbly Offered

Personal information: Employed in a management position with a large company. Forty-nine years of age.

My feelings these days:

Even though I have been taught that I shouldn't depend on things, I want to cling to something.

Even though I have been taught that I shouldn't seek form either, I want something I can see.

Even though I have been taught that work is not everything, I aim for constantly higher levels of performance.

I feel it is not right if I don't seek something and work my hardest at it.

I have decided on goals for my work that I cannot attain, while suspecting that they are exaggerated or fanciful.

Therefore, I am always tired.

I want a break.

However, if I'm not moving, with my eyes fixed firmly on the future, I feel that I will slip down from something.

If I try to unburden myself and relax, I just become that much tenser.

I want to feel good.

Although it should be close at hand, right in front of my eyes, I don't have the energy to grasp it.

I don't have the courage to bare myself.

If I bare myself, I am afraid that I will be looked down on and will lose something.

Because I've felt that I was lacking, more than others, I've always set my sights higher.

Now within the company organization, I feel I am on a level with others.

I am a manager. I even have some people under me. I am a leader.

But, now, I am tired and want to rest.

Really.

I want to draw the picture that I want and converse with the beauty of nature.

What whimpering.

However, I do feel that I would like to put a little more life back into myself.

This book, which came to my attention in my discontent, was forceful.

I want to learn more.

I want to understand more deeply about spirituality.

I am a forty-nine-year-old male, yearning to make himself shine.

This book has warned me.

However, I don't know specifically what to do. I want to know.

I want to talk about it with someone.

These are my impressions.

It would be wonderful if someone could enlighten me.

This letter illustrates the mixture of awareness, confusion, and yearning that is common in individuals who are on the threshold of a new level of spiritual exploration. The writer's reflection is filled with questions about the spiritual journey: What's really happening in my life? What am I missing? Where do I need to go from here? How do I get there? These are questions all of us face.

How Do I . . . ?

What is it that I keep missing on my journey?
What lesson do I not see?

The inner journey to discover one's spiritual core is never easy. Along the way, signposts and clues provide direction. Yet often our attention is so riveted on where we are trying to go that we miss the small, often intangible signs that might lead us to our personal treasure store. An authentic journey is not literal but metaphoric, a discovery. As Maria tells Steve, it's not like a trip to Chicago—a straight-line trip to a known destination. Looking for concrete lessons misses the point.

If you're not learning, you may need to look harder and risk more. The journey will bring few lessons if you never leave home. This letter from Dan, a U.S. health care consultant, reveals an individual who is beginning to realize it's time for him to move beyond his comfort zone:

> I have a good job, live in a beautiful neighborhood, and own a wonderful home. I have a loving wife, and two terrific kids. The other day on the way to work, I realized that my heart is not into what I am doing. I sort of hit the wall, a real personal crisis. The next day I drove to Atlanta to talk to my best friend. He gave me a copy

of *Leading with Soul*. I took it home with me and put it on the night stand behind my bed. The next night I could not get to sleep. I picked up the book and took it to the living room. I read it from cover to cover. It was a very moving experience. I got up and walked through the darkened house. I realized how much I had missed. I went back to the bedroom and woke up my wife. I said, "Honey, I have not been here for you and the kids. From now on things are going to be different." The next day I resigned my job. I'm not exactly sure what I will be doing. But a scary journey feels much better than a meaningless job and an empty life.

Even before he encountered *Leading with Soul,* Dan knew something was wrong. The book confirmed his dawning intuition that it was time to move in new directions. Because it came along at just the right time, it helped him to structure and deepen the quest he already knew, even if dimly, he had to undertake.

Where do I find a Maria—my own spiritual guide?

The simplest answer is look and you will probably find. An old Buddhist saying tells us, "When the pupil is ready, the teacher will appear." How does the pupil get ready? There is truth in the proverb "the Lord helps those who help themselves." But there is an equally important truth in the biblical injunction "they that wait upon the Lord shall renew their strength."[2] We need to be active in looking for a teacher, but we must also let go of the pride and defenses that cause us to insist that we can take care of ourselves and need no help from anyone else. Until we're ready to acknowledge our weakness, vulnerability, and incompleteness, we are not likely to find our own Maria.

Having accepted ourselves as we are, we still have to get out and look. "Ask, and it will be given you; seek, and you will find; knock, and it will be opened to you."[3] If you're not finding your own Maria where you've been looking, expand your options. Get involved in new activities or groups. Look for the right *spiritual home.* Sometimes that's as simple as searching out the right church or temple. Other times it might mean getting involved in community or charitable activities that deepen your growth and bring you into contact with new people. But the key is to be both receptive and active. Take time to be with yourself and to pray or meditate as well as taking time to be with others to learn and grow. Open yourself to possibilities—life abounds with teachers and lessons.

There must be many guides out there because many readers have written to say they know a Maria. Of course these guides have many different names, and they are remarkably diverse in age, profession, gender, and just about everything else. The challenge is finding someone who cares enough about us and our development to be willing to offer an optimal blend of love and challenge. Sometimes two people can do that for one another— as in some marriages.

How can we become more aware of the spiritual guides
that come in and out of our lives and embrace them
rather than put them off?
We need to listen to those small, still inner voices that call our attention to things outside our normal awareness. We also need to pay attention when day-to-day experiences—such as conversations at work, over a meal, or at a social event—trigger thoughts or images that might take us somewhere important if we follow them where they lead. Stories, in particular, help us see things we would otherwise miss. Jackie Shrago, business executive, wrote to describe this insight that hit her in response to a story in the book:

> The woman's story about a stream in chapter four struck
> a chord that described my own journey. The business
> that I co-founded had been my stream of life for ten

years. It embodied the profession I had developed, all of my creative energy, my family, even my soul. And then, I sold my share of the business and signed a no-compete agreement. Suddenly in 1986, with my signature on those agreements, just like the stream I arrived at a desert. I no longer knew who I was. I had lost all the ways in which I had defined myself. The wind called, but I didn't know how to give up who I had been. All were gone: my profession, my daily activities, my family. I had to identify anew the essence of my soul and give in to the wind and the desert to find myself on the other side. Gradually my technology experience, my early passion for teaching, and my political experience during the desert years emerged and blended together in a new stream to create new opportunities in the emerging field of the Internet. By 1991, there was again a stream flowing in my life, with direction and focus. Without giving in to the desert and the wind it would have been difficult if not impossible to imagine the new beginning, reclaim my soul, and identify the new stream of life. Thanks for helping me put words to my story and my journey.

As a middle manager I feel strangled. I feel I'm on a leash, and I get jerked back if I step out too far. How do I lead with soul when I don't feel it from above?

When you're in the middle—and most of us are one way or another—feeling trapped comes naturally. You're expected to follow directives from above and ensure that sometimes unwilling subordinates comply and get things done. It's easy to feel like a yo-yo—bouncing first one way then another, depending on who's pulling your string.

If your workplace or your boss is hopelessly toxic, ask whether hanging on is really your best option. Moving on is often the first step to spiritual development. But no workplace is perfect, and leading with soul offers a way out of feeling trapped. The less you're in touch with who you are, what you value, and what you believe, the more you're vulnerable to feeling lost and adrift, easily pushed this way and that by the pressures around you. But as you identify your spiritual center and learn to lead from your heart, you have a solid base from which you can influence up and inspire down. Granted, it's not risk free. Telling the truth and standing firmly for what you believe won't always win friends. Sometimes people may question whether you're a team player.

But don't give in too easily to fear of being the nail that stands up and gets pounded. The consequences are often continuing fear and conformity, which are as bad for organizations as for individuals. Yes, you could get canned, though the risk of that is often overrated. Risk needs to be balanced against the many stories of courage and integrity that have produced huge dividends in the long run. If you need to, you can probably find a better job elsewhere. And you might even get promoted by your current employer. Either way you will feel better and more fulfilled. You may delight in the joy of making a difference, and your integrity will be intact. Not a bad legacy to pass on.

Kristin Ragusin, a financial consultant with one of America's biggest stockbrokers, illustrates elegantly the possibilities that are unleashed when a single individual finds ways to integrate spirituality with work. Asked if there wasn't a conflict between the bottom-line focus of her profession and her spirituality, she responded:

> I don't see life divided like that. My work is a continual voyage of self-discovery. There's nothing like money to reveal people's values and their sense of meaning. My engagement with clients brings up the deepest questions. Who am I? Who are these people? Often they come in

scared, excited, happy, guilty, all at once. Then financial planning is itself a process of self-discovery—where are your priorities, what do you want to do in retirement? People are generally uncomfortable with knowing who they are other than as consumers of the American capitalist myth. I know that consumerism is filling a black hole inside, so I listen for the signs of that in their story. In them, I see the richness of who we all are, how our core issues are all the same.[4]

Ragusin understands that financial planning is about money, but she is wise enough to see that it's also about things even more important than money. "When a new client comes in, I simply hold the questions: Who is this soul? What does he or she cherish? That's where I go now, and the plan is simple then."[5] She has also found that the clearer she has become about the spiritual dimension in her work, the easier the work itself has become and the more successful she has been.

I believe that leadership involves the giving of gifts, but I worry about how people will respond. Aren't there some tensions here?
In gift giving, as in most of the interesting things in life, there are dilemmas. Giving authorship creates opportunities for people to

put their signature on their work but individual priorities can undermine organization-wide standards. Consumers expect consistency in goods and services and become upset when their expectations are not met. Giving people power carries risks. There is always someone who will take advantage of having clout. The gift of love extends caring and compassion, but what do you do when tough decisions need to be made that will affect people's lives and livelihoods? Trying to create an organization that infuses work with a deeply felt sense of significance flies in the face of today's widespread cynicism. People may interpret the gift of significance as another round of management manipulation. Steve Camden experienced firsthand many of these dilemmas, sometimes painfully. Maria's coaching helped, but the key was that he kept trying and learned from his mistakes.

It's important to recognize the risks and dilemmas because then you're less likely to be startled or discouraged when you trip over them occasionally. We'll fail for sure if our gifts are half-hearted or inauthentic. But as we continue our spiritual journey, we acquire new gifts and increase our capacity to give to others. As we deepen our own faith, we understand even more deeply that we need to offer our gifts to others for their sake as well as our own.

How do you lead difficult employees?

Leadership would be easier if everyone around us was cooper-
ative, upbeat, and a joy to work with. But most workplaces contain at least a few people who seem close to impossible. When
we encounter difficult people, we often assume that the problem is them. But it's often the case that people who seem difficult are really having problems with their work situation. We
seem preprogrammed to blame people rather than to focus on
what in people's environment may be causing the problem.
That's where leadership gifts can help. Sometimes, difficult people don't believe anyone really cares about them, and they may
not realize their actions keep people at a distance. In such cases
even a modest dose of caring and compassion can make a surprising difference.

Other times, people feel no sense of real accomplishment, of
seeing how their efforts produce something they can be proud
of. Many progressive employers have found that giving more
opportunities for authorship can transform complainers into
engaged workers. We've all heard that power corrupts, but powerlessness is even more corrosive. People who feel powerless are
almost always pains in the butt to those with power. Sharing
power goes a long way toward letting people know that they can

have some clout in making a better work environment. People are also likely to become difficult when they feel their life and work have no real meaning. That's where the gift of significance can work magic. Even the most disgruntled employee can sign on to accomplish something that makes sense to him or her or can get caught up in the spirit of authentic ritual, ceremony, or stories. So the next time you find yourself labeling someone as difficult, look around you or look in the mirror for the root cause.

How can I use Leading with Soul to foster a dialogue with friends or coworkers?

Readers have often asked how to break the ice and start discussing soul and spirit. There are many paths to a deeper conversation, and each group needs to find the route that works for it. But here are a few possibilities that have worked for the authors or other readers.

1. Sometimes, it helps to begin by talking about someone else. For example, people who have read *Leading with Soul* can talk about their reactions to the story and the characters. What parts of the story do they like best? Which do they like least? How do they react to Steve? To Maria? Do they identify more with one or the other? What's bothering Steve when he first meets Maria?

How does she respond? Is she helpful or not? Why, for example, does Maria tell Steve to get lost? Is that good advice or bad? What happens for Steve when he tries to follow it?

In talking about Steve and Maria, people naturally glide into reflecting on themselves as well. The differences in the ways individuals see the characters and the story are important and fruitful sources of learning, particularly when people avoid the temptation to defend their own interpretations and to foist them on others. If, for example, one person is drawn to Steve Camden but another sees him as weak and confused, the different perceptions probably say more about the two individuals than about the character in the book. Both of them might learn from a dialogue about their differing perceptions.

2. Look for ways to use expressive, or "soulful," media such as drama, poetry, music, and art. Some groups have focused on the poems in *Leading with Soul*. Ask people to choose the poem they like best. Individuals can read aloud the poems they have selected and talk about what the poems say. A comfortable room, candles, and music in the background can all add to the mood.

3. Showing segments of videos or feature films can be an avenue to powerful discussions. The better or more popular a film, the more likely it is to contain important messages about life, love, leadership, and the spiritual journey. This is true of box

office sensations such as *Titanic, The Lion King, The Godfather* (I and II), and the original *Star Wars* trilogy. It's true of classics like *It's a Wonderful Life, To Kill a Mockingbird,* and *Citizen Kane.* Powerful stories of leadership and soul can be found in films like *Gandhi, Schindler's List,* and *Mr. Smith Goes to Washington.*

  4. Storytelling is a powerful medium. Individuals can compose stories about their life journey, focusing on the people, places, and events that have influenced their understanding of leadership. Groups can also tell stories about themselves and the organization, as they did in Steve Camden's organization at company gatherings.

Spreading Spirit

Has fact-driven, scientifically oriented, rigorous education created a cohort of students who simply cannot comprehend or relate to the language of soul and spirit?

Scratch and sniff beneath their self-assured and rational veneers, and you find that many of today's students are searching for deeper, more fulfilling, and more meaningful lives. Their journeys are often taken alone and rarely shared with others because these young people think they need to mask this personal search from others. When they're given the opportunity to drop their masks and share their inner thoughts, pains, and passions with others, they relish the connection. But where do they typically get the chance? Rarely in classrooms. Sometimes in enlightened companies. Most often in more informal settings—sororities and fraternities, sports teams, or even gangs. Good education needs to balance mind and soul, head and heart.

As the use of temporary workers to reduce costs and increase flexibility becomes a more prominent practice, how can spirited leaders draw these short-termers into the fold?

Part of the answer here is to be bone-honest about the nature of the relationship. It may not be a long-term marriage, but it can be a mutually rewarding short-term love affair. Robert Waterman has characterized the modern employee-employer relationship as one in which the boss promises a fair wage, a rewarding job, the best training available, and respect. The employee reciprocates with hard work, high commitment, and temporary loyalty. When the relationship is terminated, it is done with caring, compassion, and assurance that the employees will land a job someplace else and that the employer will not have to worry about client poaching or trading of competitive secrets.[6] Tracy Kidder has described how both workers and bosses poured heart and soul into the development of a new computer. At the end the group disbanded, but even though the individuals went their separate ways, they carried with them pride in accomplishing a difficult task and the promise of relationships that would last a lifetime. As Dan West, one of the group's leaders, commented: "It was a summer romance. But that's all right. Summer romances are some of the best things that ever happen."[7]

How do leaders help teachers become believers in their potential and their capacity to change?

We have all heard from teachers and school administrators how hard it is to keep the faith in the face of almost overwhelming challenges and sometimes lukewarm public support. Too often teachers are told that the content they transmit is far more important than who they are. But most of us have had a teacher somewhere along the line who made a profound and positive difference. We may or may not remember much of the information that teacher passed along, but we remember a caring human being who chose to invest in our learning. As Tracy Kidder has observed:

> Teachers usually have no way of knowing that they have made a difference in a child's life, even when they have made a dramatic one. But for children who are used to thinking of themselves as stupid or not worth

talking to or deserving rape and beatings, a good teacher can provide an astonishing revelation. A good teacher can give a child at least a chance to feel "She thinks I'm worth something, maybe I am." Good teachers put snags in the river of children passing by, and over the years, they redirect hundreds of lives. Many people find it easy to imagine unseen webs of malevolent conspiracy in the world, and they are not always wrong. But there is also an innocence that conspires to hold humanity together, and it is made up of people who can never fully know that good they have done.[8]

Leaders can help teachers acknowledge and appreciate this good that they do. Indeed, this is an issue not just for teachers but also for many other workers who wonder if they are getting anything done or if their work really makes a difference. These are essentially problems of significance. The challenge for leaders is to go beyond a focus on day-to-day management concerns and crises and to focus on the larger purpose of work and of the institution in which the work is carried out. Budgets have to be balanced and paper has to be pushed, but that's the easy part of being a manager or a schoolteacher. The deeper and more important task is to give passionate, relentless attention to mission and purpose, continually seeking ways to offer the gift of significance to one's constituents.

Are you yourselves currently involved in spirituality programs? Both of us are involved regularly in seminars that feature ideas drawn from this book. But we're only a small part of a much larger movement. Many individuals and organizations are engaged in activities designed to bring soul and spirit into work. The Robert K. Greenleaf Center in Indianapolis[9] has an active program on *servant leadership* that takes seriously the spiritual dimension in organizations. The annual Conference on Business and Consciousness,[10] held every year on the Pacific coast of Mexico, has been exploring issues of spirituality at work for more than five years. The program features academics, authors, and business executives who are trying to create a more soulful work environment. Beginning with only about three hundred participants in its first year, the conference has grown dramatically since.

A growing number of organizations are developing their own internal programs to explore the spiritual dimension. Prince Philipp of Liechtenstein, chairman of Liechtenstein Global Trust, has created a leadership academy for his international group of financial managers. For three weeks, participants create art, take

Aikido lessons, learn to juggle, and take part in a rich set of expressive experiences. Prince Philipp told us, "I already have very good managers. But in today's world our company needs really good leaders. To lead, you've got to be in touch with your heart and soul."[11] We believe that the business world will see more programs like this in the future.

Have you thought about pulling together a group of people to share stories about their personal journeys and experiences at work?

Since *Leading with Soul* was published, we frequently convene occasions for people to share stories about their personal journeys or about the joys and trials, the ups and downs of life at work. The energy, humor, and poignancy such events draw forth offer us constant delight. It has been said that God created humans because he loves stories. Our experiences show that it's true.

Soul at Work

Does the real world offer leaders like Maria and Steve? Are there really workplaces that take soul and spirit seriously? Some of our readers have their doubts. "I love the idea of more soulful and spirited workplaces," one Dutch reader told us, "but this vision might be too beautiful for this hard world." A reader in California commented, "The book describes a leader with strong spiritual convictions, giving and loving. But how such a leader can survive the harsh business reality is not clear to me."

Such doubts are no surprise. Business realities are often very harsh. Yet we encounter more and more examples that show a spiritual renaissance in the workplace is not only possible, it's already happening. Here's one, from the *Kansas City Star:*

They showed *Sister Act* movie clips of Whoopi Goldberg cultivating a choir of nuns. A guy in a tuxedo talked about spirit at work. Six persons brandished noise-makers and stood to reflect on "heart" and "power" and the golden rule.

A couple of years ago, Ford plant manager Gerry Minor began holding Friday afternoon leadership meetings to share information and management training. Anyone in the plant is welcome to attend. Regular features include a "business acumen" presentation that shares financial or business information. Last week's session, for example, emphasized the financial imprint of the plant, which employs 4,880 hourly and 342 salaried workers.

Also on the agenda are discussions of reading material Minor assigns. Last week the focus was on *Leading with Soul,* an allegory about a search for meaning in life and work, written by Lee Bolman and Terry Deal.

Joe Williams, a financial analyst who spent 11 years on the assembly line before getting a college degree and moving into the plant's finance office, wore a tux as the book report's master of ceremonies.

"We wanted to have fun," Williams said of the reviewers, who were first-line supervisors and midlevel plant managers. They read the book and shared their reactions, interspersed with *Sister Act* clips showing the step-by-step transformation of a dismal choir into crowd-pleasing performers.

"We brainstormed," Williams said. "We talked about what the book meant to us. Different people took different things from it, and we just tried to share those feelings."

When Minor first convened the Friday afternoon meetings, those who attended were quiet and came mostly to observe. Over the months, staff involvement has grown. Inhibitions have waned. The evolution played out Friday.

"We have seen the power of shared emotion, of creating a common spirit," Minor said after the review group's presentation. Minor wouldn't mind if shared spirit is his legacy at the plant, which became Ford's largest-volume manufacturing site under his tenure.[1]

You might think an old Ford plant in Claycomo, Missouri, would be one of the last places in the world to put *Leading with*

Soul on its reading list. Yet that kind of unorthodox approach helped plant manager Gerry Minor and his colleagues build the Claycomo facility into one of the largest and most successful auto assembly plants in the world.

This is not an isolated example. Since *Leading with Soul* was published, we've received calls and letters from people all over the world who have been getting together with coworkers to explore the implications of the book for their own organization. Among the organizations have been a hotel in Jakarta, an oil company in Texas, a nonprofit in Michigan, and a consumer products company in Japan.

We have also been gratified by the enormous interest in spiritual issues that we have found in school districts across America. One fascinating example of this has been occurring in Lawndale, California. The Lawndale Elementary School District might seem an unlikely candidate for a spiritual renaissance. It is located in a poor town just south of the Los Angeles airport, and 91 percent of its students are minorities, 84 percent receive free or reduced-price lunches, and 20 percent are transients. To make things even more difficult the district's staff is 91 percent white.

Several years ago the superintendent, Joe Condon, and one of the district's principals, Dorinda Dee, got together after the summer recess. Each had a book to recommend to the other. They were surprised to learn that their recommendations were identical—*Leading with Soul.* The superintendent soon bought the book for each of the system's principals. The leadership team, consisting of the superintendent and the principals, used it as a basis for a series of discussions. For some principals the ideas reinforced what they already believed, provided a common vocabulary, and helped build a stronger sense of community. For other administrators, those who had narrower views of their role, the ideas felt foreign. They had difficulty connecting with others in the group. Some principals left the district. Even today, according to Condon, people who cannot connect to others or to the spirit of the job will not "find a match in Lawndale."

The first part of the team's discussion centered on people's personal journeys. Frank Noyes, a principal, observed: "The book became a tool to look at ourselves and then at how we could connect more closely to our lives at work. We realized that when you tap into your soul you realize that you have personal gifts to share and then can offer them to the wider community." From the leadership team the ideas began to wend into the Lawndale district culture. Some of the discussions were one-on-one; others were in small groups. Teachers especially were drawn into the dialogues. A principal remarked: "Teachers have life issues going on when teaching. If a teacher dries up, he or she can't help others. People learned they have to take care of themselves to do a good job. The real meaning of leading with soul is what teaching is all about. Maria was Steve's teacher."

At a recent symposium to kick off the school year for the entire district staff, *Leading with Soul* was shared with custodians, secretaries, and other classified employees as well as certificated personnel. In small groups, they all discussed the interlude "Community and the Cycle of Giving." They were asked to highlight things that spoke to them and then to discuss how gift giving could enhance the Lawndale community in the coming year. There was an open discussion of love and "how we can express love for one another." Following the discussion a modified game of *Jeopardy* helped newcomers learn the cultural history of the district. The plan was to follow up the retreat with "family" groups that would meet throughout the school year to focus on other sections of the book. Dorinda Dee captured the soulful strategy: "This is our way of bringing the whole side of life into balance—caring, authorship, and power give significance to what we do. To work is to live; to live is to work."

Superintendent Condon summed up the emerging spirit of Lawndale: "In my annual report to the school board, not one word was spent on goals or test scores. We focused on what people are bringing to the party. This goes much deeper than work. It gets at the essence of who we are. We have to deal with that before we start to work."[2]

Lawndale and the Claycomo Ford plant are only two of the many examples cropping up not only in North America but around the world. Our colleague Philip Mirvis was kind enough to share his experiences in working with a fascinating company in the Netherlands:

> When Tex Gunning took charge in late 1995 of Van den Bergh Foods, a Dutch subsidiary of Unilever, he made all the right moves: an analysis of current problems and opportunities, the start of a bold change program to turn around lackluster performance, and the launch of successful new products into the marketplace. But something was missing. At a management meeting in late 1997 participants agreed that business was good, but the company lacked "heart." Their aspiration was to *reconnect* deeply—intellectually and emotionally—to each other and to customers.
>
> Working with me and a team of group facilitators from the Foundation for Community Encouragement,

Tex led a series of retreats with roughly 200 leaders at all levels in the company. In 1998, all 200 bicycled and camped together in the Ardennes Forest in Belgium. In an ancient monastery, Tex shared his emotional lifeline— a story of experiences, both highs and lows—from childhood to the present. Leaders then shared their own stories with two or three peers. In the next two days, they met in moments of silent reflection and in open dialogues about their work and the business. A collective commitment was made to "be authentic" with one other, to listen deeply, and to "deal with difficult issues."

As a follow-up, the 200 participated in a company-wide learning conference with all 2,400 of their employees, who also shared life histories and talked about themselves and their work. One manager summed up the impact: "For me it represented a major turnaround . . . the way leaders and then all the people of Van den Bergh showed something personal about themselves. The example showed that I am more than just a 'working' person in the company. The 'whole' person is welcomed."

In 1999, Tex and his team of 200 met in Scotland— this time to hike together and talk about their legacy. Shortly thereafter, they met with 10,000 customers in a stadium to deal openly with difficult issues and talk about their lives and work.

In 2000, the venue was the desert of Jordan—a base for dialogues about lessons learned and for a ceremony in the ancient city of Petra to celebrate accomplishments. Managers rode camels and shared their appreciation and good wishes with Tex, who was about to move to a new job. There was much to cheer: double-digit growth in previously flat markets and record profitability. Even in the flickering torchlight, those present could see the tears on Tex's cheeks as he said, "The real miracle is that we have turned ourselves into a community."[3]

Bringing soul to work goes well beyond these three examples. Other individuals and organizations are evolving their own distinctive approaches to leading with soul. In many of these efforts, leaders offer their unique and personal versions of the four gifts discussed in this book—authorship, love, power, and significance.

The Gift of Authorship

University classrooms are often places where the teacher issues commands that students dutifully follow: "Do what you are told, work hard, and a good grade will be your reward." Too often this results in assignments students hate doing and instructors loathe grading. But one professor told us about the surprising things he found happening when he tried to offer authorship to a group of students enrolled in a senior seminar:

> Year after year, I've given students specific instructions for the assignments I'd ask them to do. They would comply, and I would feel in complete control. But they never seemed really excited about what they were doing. And I was rarely very impressed with what they had done. *Leading with Soul* offered a new possibility: why not give them a chance to create something on their own. So rather than a specific assignment, I assigned a rather amorphous task—a reflective essay. But as time went on, I was very disappointed in the results. No one seemed to be doing anything. As the semester drew to a close, I grew more and more angry. At the last class, I decided to vent my frustration. The students had taken advantage of my gift and I wanted them to know how it felt to be ripped off.
>
> As I was preparing to launch my diatribe, one of the students raised her hand and asked when they could share their personal growth projects. I told her I

did not assign a personal growth project. She told me the class had gotten together and figured out what I really meant by "reflective essay." They then shared what they had done.

I was completely blown away by their accomplishments: art, poetry, and other attempts to capture the essence of leadership. One student remarked that he learned that leadership was as much about reflection as about action. His personal growth project was to design and build a bench where students could sit and reflect, because he had observed that there was no place like that on campus. That bench is now a popular spot where students can sit and ponder the meaning of life. Another student was disturbed about a university tradition that had been discarded. When her mother graduated, students received an iris bulb as a symbol that their knowledge gained would continue to grow. Her mother's rhizome had eventually become a large iris bed that was a source of real family pride. As her personal growth project, the student went to some of the wealthy graduates of the university. She asked for donations to make it possible for each of the graduating seniors to receive an iris during commencement activities. Her efforts became part of a front page article in the university newspaper. When that news came to the attention of the faculty commencement committee she was summoned to appear. Her plan flew in the face of a university rule that prohibited any kind of adornment at graduation. But she was determined and willing to risk whatever punishment would befall her if she carried out her plan.

The day of graduation the seniors marched in carrying their beautiful blue irises. During his speech, the university chancellor commented on what the student had done and read a letter from an alumnus whose heart had been deeply moved by the renewal of an old tradition. As he spoke, all the seniors raised their irises high. The student's personal growth project had made a real difference. Later on, the student called me and asked if she had learned the right lesson from her experience: "As a leader, you do what you think is right and stand prepared to take the heat so that good things can happen."

Those are only two examples of what my gift of authorship yielded. Even in my wildest dreams I would never have imagined what students could do if given the chance.

The same lesson applies to employees, wherever they work. What people can do by following the rules and doing what they're told pales in significance compared to what they can accomplish when given the opportunity to put their signature on their work. More and more companies are now taking notice: cut employees some slack, encourage them to think, and watch what they produce on their own without direction from the top.

The Gift of Love

If you doubt that love can have a place in a modern corporation, try telling it to Herb Kelleher, the one-of-a-kind CEO of Southwest Airlines. When asked what has made Southwest so successful, he talks about people, humor, love, and soul. Simply put, Kelleher "cherishes and respects" his eighteen thousand employees, and his "love" is returned in what he calls "a spontaneous, voluntary overflowing of emotion."[4]

They talk openly about love at Southwest Airlines: they fly out of Love Field in Dallas, their symbol on the New York Stock Exchange is LUV, the employee newsletter is called *Luv Line,* and their twentieth anniversary slogan was "20 Years of Loving You."[5] They hold an annual Heroes of the Heart ceremony to honor people behind the scenes who have gone above and beyond even Southwest's high standards of duty. There are, of course, ups and downs in any family, and the airline industry certainly brings both good days and bad. Through life's peaks and valleys, love holds people together in a caring community. A Southwest employee has said, "Herb loves us. We love Herb. We love one another. We love the company. One of the primary beneficiaries of our collective caring is our passengers."[6]

Spiritual message? Love? From a CEO who is renowned for his attraction to cigarettes and bourbon? Is there any reason to treat this as more than an outlying fluke? There are plenty of skeptics. A competing airline executive has grumbled, "Southwest runs on Herb's bullshit."[7] But there are many other successful leaders who embrace a philosophy much like Kelleher's. Ben Cohen, cofounder of the ice cream company Ben and Jerry's Homemade, observes: "Businesses tend to exploit communities and their workers, and that wasn't the way I thought the game should be played. I thought it should be the opposite—that because the business is allowed to be there in the first place, the business ought to support the community. What we're finding is that when you support the community, the community supports you back. When you give love, you receive love. I maintain that there is a spiritual dimension to business just as there is to the lives of individuals."[8]

An understated counterpoint to Kelleher's high jinks is the caring shown by Aaron Feuerstein, president of textile manufacturer Malden Mills. Feuerstein astounded everyone, most of all his workforce, after fire wiped out most of his plant in December 1995. The next day, he announced that all three thousand of his workers would remain on the payroll for the following month. In January, he announced he would pay them for another month, and he extended the offer again in February. "The second time was a shock. It was the third time that brought tears to everyone's eyes." By March, most of his employees were back on the job. Feuerstein's generosity went against the advice of members of his board and cost him several million dollars. But he felt a responsibility to both workers and community. He quoted Hillel, a first-century Talmudic scholar: "Not all who increase their wealth are wise." Said Feuerstein, "If you think the only function of a CEO is to increase the wealth of shareholders, then any time he spends on Scripture or Shakespeare or the arts is wasteful. But if you think the CEO must balance responsibilities, then he should be involved with ideas that connect him with the past, the present and the future."

Despite unusually bad winter weather, Malden Mills was back in production faster than anyone expected. "Our people became very creative," said Feuerstein. "They were willing to work 25 hours a day."[9]

Even in the intensely competitive, sometimes violent world of professional sports, outstanding teams regularly use images of family, spirit, and love to explain their success. After professional football's 2001 Super Bowl, the owner of the winning Baltimore Ravens gave credit to the team's "chemistry". "There's a lot of love on this team," he said. "And Vince Lombardi told me that years ago. In order to win, you have to love each other."[10]

The Gift of Power

Examples are multiplying of organizations that have found the power of giving power. You can see it in many of the companies that make *Fortune's* annual list of the one hundred best places to work in America. For example, the gift of power is central to the *open-book management* movement, inspired particularly by Jack Stack of Springfield Remanufacturing. Stack tells a persuasive story of turning around a moribund manufacturing company in Missouri by giving employees as much financial information as possible so that they began to think and act like owners. Stack's "ultimate higher law" is that you get the highest level of performance when you appeal to the highest level of thinking. The success of that philosophy has since been replicated in many other organizations.[11]

Another old company that fell on hard times before reinventing itself through employee empowerment is Harley-Davidson. To aficionados, a "Harley" has always been more than just a motorcycle. It is a link to a long and proud tradition and qualifies its owner as a member of a special fraternity—HOG, the Harley Owners Group. By the early 1980s, though, this venerable American institution was on the ropes, brought to its knees by high costs, poor quality, and intense foreign competition. Intending to be a white knight, American Machine and Foundry bought the company, but this proved an unhelpful alliance and ended with an internal buyout of Harley-Davidson by a group of Harley executives.

The question the new owners faced was how to save the company. Their conclusion: people were Harley's most important resource. But how could this valuable resource be activated? One alternative was to spread the potential wealth through attractive compensation packages. But another alternative seemed even more promising—give employees some clout in shaping the company's direction and operations.

Historically, Harley-Davidson management had evidenced a command-and-control mentality. The top made all the decisions, and the bottom carried them out. The new regime turned the old approach on its head. It gave employees a say in determining all aspects of the company, from vision and values to policies and procedures. Despite all the expected ups and downs (akin to those Steve Camden experienced in making a gift of power to his operation), Harley subsequently went on a roll. Market share jumped from 15 to 50 percent. Revenue and employees more than doubled. Production tripled. In sum, Harley got itself on the move again. In giving power to the company's human capital, a struggling enterprise once again became a thriving institution.[12]

Another subtle but profound example of an organization that has discovered how to use the gift of power is Alcoholics Anonymous. AA's twelve-step program has achieved extraordinary success in helping addicts escape alcohol dependence. Its emphasis on spirituality has worked where professionalism and expertise have often failed. AA gives power paradoxically. The first of its twelve steps asks addicts to make this acknowledgment: "We are powerless over alcohol, and our lives have become unmanageable." The second step is to accept that there is a "power greater than ourselves" that can "restore us to sanity." The third is to turn "our wills and our lives over to the care of God as we understand him." The eleventh step asks the addict to pray "only for knowledge of his will for us and the power to carry that out." The path to power, in AA's view the *only* path, begins with admitting powerlessness and putting oneself in the hands of a higher power.

But AA does not expect individuals to find and follow this path on their own. They learn about it from other recovering addicts. In AA, everyone teaches and everyone learns. All must rely on God, but every individual is a vehicle not just for carrying out God's will but for empowering others to carry it out as well.

Modern organizations are increasingly recognizing the power of AA's basic message. The more individuals try to go it alone and rely solely on themselves, the more powerless they will be. The path to power and empowerment requires deep understanding that each of us is finite and needs to seek and welcome help from beyond ourselves.

The Gift of Significance

Medtronic, a highly successful, multinational health care firm, like many similarly successful organizations, looks beyond the bottom line to focus on its deeper mission. That mission gives significance to everything Medtronic's people do. Bill George, the chief executive of Medtronic, explains the firm's spiritual underpinnings this way:

> Medtronic was founded more than forty years ago by a spiritual leader named Earl Bakken. Sure Earl is a great inventor who created the first battery-operated wearable pacemaker. He also is a great visionary who in

1960, when the company was near bankruptcy, wrote a mission statement that laid out Medtronic's future for the next hundred years. But even more important than that, Earl is still the spiritual leader, or "soul," of Medtronic, despite the fact that he has been retired for four years.

The mission he wrote more than thirty years ago, not one word of which has been changed, calls for Medtronic to restore people to the fullness of life and health. Our 9,000 employees are totally dedicated to that mission, regardless of whether they work in the R&D lab, the factory, the accounting department, or in the hospital. What are these values? They are, first of all, restoring people to full health; next, serving our customer with products and services of unsurpassed quality; recognizing the personal worth of employees; making a fair profit and return for our shareholders; and maintaining good citizenship as a company. And the results of the past thirty years, or the past eight years, seem to validate that approach: $1,000 invested in 1960 in Medtronic stock would be worth $1.65 million today. At Medtronic, we don't mix religion and business, but we certainly do not shy away from the spiritual side of our work and the deeper meaning of our mission to save lives.[13]

Medtronic is far from unique in putting significance at its core. Merck & Company, one of the world's most successful pharmaceutical firms, states its core purpose in terms very similar to Medtronic's: "preserving and improving human life." Is such a statement more than words? Do noble-sounding sentiments really make a difference in key decisions and everyday behavior? In Merck's case, the answer is yes. The company points proudly to instances in which it sold a drug at a loss or gave it away to fulfill the core value of putting patients first. In one famous example, Merck had to decide whether to develop and distribute a drug for river-blindness, an affliction of the poor in many Third World countries. Cost-benefit analysis was clear—the drug had little chance of making money. For companies with eyes fixed on the bottom line, such a decision would be a no-brainer. Merck developed the drug anyway and then gave it away. Merck's chief executive officer said the decision was easy because the company's purpose was clear, and many of its key employees would have been demoralized had it not chosen not to honor its mission.

Conclusion

A growing number of organizations in business and elsewhere are exploring soul and spirit in ways that create bonds, kindle passion, and give meaning to work. These organizations are finding unique and creative ways to offer gifts like authorship, love, power, and significance.

Sometimes, all it takes is a simple act of caring by one individual. Our friend John Jacobson shared this simple, but powerful example:

> When I was a principal, a first-grade child, Cheryl, lost her mother to cancer. As she dealt with this tragic loss, she turned to writing as a source of comfort and an outlet for her feelings and emotions. Upon completion of her writing, the teacher asked Cheryl if she wanted to share her writing with the class. In this first-grade classroom, the sharing of writing was an everyday occurrence at the end of the writing workshop. During this sharing time, one child generally sat in an author's chair in the front of the class with the other children gathered around on the carpet. On this particular day, the teacher, sensitive to Cheryl's feelings, asked if she would like to sit on his lap. As Cheryl shared her thoughts with the class

while sitting securely on her teacher's lap, hearts were touched, and the class bonded in spirit.[14]

All four gifts were exchanged in this one simple encounter. What better way to experience authorship than to sit in the author's chair and share one's own writing? The offer of a lap to sit on exemplifies the possibilities for love that we often miss in daily life. Writing about one's feelings and experiences and then sharing them with friends are powerful ways to find meaning and significance and to begin to exert some power over any demons that might be haunting one.

The possibilities for giving these gifts and leading with soul are all around us if we look for them. Sometimes all it takes is a simple gesture. At other times it requires all the passion, courage, and caring that we can muster. Yet as the examples in this chapter suggest, the potential rewards are great.

"I wear the chains I forged in life," says Marley's ghost in Charles Dickens's *A Christmas Carol*. Each of us every day builds a legacy we will leave behind, our contribution to humankind . . . Though we may not admit it even to ourselves, many of us live as if hoping to be remembered for the size of a house, the name-plate on a car, or a rung attained on a corporate ladder. Small wonder so many successful people, like Steve Camden in our story, hit a wall and wonder what happened to the meaning and zest in their lives. The world will little lament nor long remember those whose primary life achievement is material comfort or self-aggrandizement. The message of this book is simple. Your life journey is a continuing opportunity to deepen your faith, develop your gifts, and enhance your contribution to what the world becomes. At Maria's funeral (in Chapter Sixteen), Steve Camden read Rumi's poetic description of three companions. The first, your possessions, won't even leave the house when you're in danger or difficulty. The second, your good friend, will come to the funeral, but not farther. Only the third, your work—all that you do to offer your unique gifts to others—goes beyond this life "down into the grave, to help."[15] Rumi's advice is sound: take deep refuge with that companion beforehand. Unshackle the chains that weigh you down and unleash your spirit as a guide to your journey and a beacon to your fellow travelers.

NOTES

Prelude: In Search of Soul and Spirit

Epigraph: Rumi, "Who Says Word with My Mouth?" in J. Moyne and C. Barks, *Open Secret: Versions of Rumi* (Putney, Vt.: Threshold Books, 1984), p. 37. Rumi (1207–1273) was a Sufi mystic, poet, and philosopher. His full name is usually transliterated into English as Jalāl ad-Dīn ar-Rūmī or Jalaluddin Rumi. Born in what is now Afghanistan, he and his family were displaced by the Mongol invasion, relocating to an area that is now part of Turkey. Sufism is distinguished by its emphasis on religious exercises that produce a direct and personal experience of God. In the tenth through thirteenth centuries, the ablest thinkers in Islam were often Sufis. Many of them, like Rumi, developed a remarkably inclusive spirituality, not at all consistent with Western stereotypes of Muslims as zealous fundamentalists or backward provincials. Rumi founded the order that became known in the West as the Whirling Dervishes.

1. In the Gospel According to St. Mark (8:36, King James Version), for example, Mark tells us that Jesus asked, "For what shall it profit a man, if he shall gain the whole world, and lose his own soul?" See also Matthew 16:26 and Luke 9:25.

2. W. Bennis, "Foreword," in I. I. Mitroff and E. A. Denton, *A Spiritual Audit of Corporate America* (San Francisco: Jossey-Bass, 1999), p. xi.

3. M. Fox, *The Reinvention of Work: A New Vision of Livelihood for Our Time* (San Francisco: HarperSanFrancisco, 1994), pp. 1–2.

4. Statement made to the authors by Father Paul during an interview on his New York radio program, *As You Think.*

5. We have listed many of the recent books on work and spirit in the Recommended Reading section that follows these notes.

6. Compare J. Hillman, *A Blue Fire: Selected Writings,* ed. T. Moore (New York: HarperCollins, 1991), p. 113.

7. J. Hawley, *Reawakening the Spirit in Work: The Power of Dharmic Management* (San Francisco: Berrett-Koehler, 1993), p. 3.

8. W. Whitman, "Passage to India," in M. Van Doren (ed.), *The Portable Walt Whitman* (New York: Penguin, 1977), p. 284.

Interlude: Reclaiming Your Soul

Epigraph: J. Campbell, *A Joseph Campbell Companion: Reflections on the Art of Living,* ed. D. K. Osbon (New York: HarperPerennial, 1995), p. 24.

1. A. Schweitzer, quoted in P. L. Berman, *The Search for Meaning: Americans Talk About What They Believe and Why* (New York: Ballantine, 1990), p. vi.

2. R. D. Putnam, "Bowling Alone: America's Declining Social Capital," *Journal of Democracy,* 1995, *6,* 67–78.

3. R. E. Lane, *The Loss of Happiness in Market Democracies* (New Haven, Conn.: Yale University Press, 2000).

4. J. C. Collins and J. I. Porras, *Built to Last: Successful Habits of Visionary Companies* (New York: HarperBusiness, 1994).

5. S. Reynolds, *Thoughts from Chairman Buffett: Thirty Years of Unconventional Wisdom from the Sage of Omaha* (New York: HarperBusiness, 1998), p. 37.

6. 1 John 2:27, as rendered by S. Mitchell (ed.), *The Enlightened Mind: An Anthology of Sacred Prose* (New York: HarperCollins, 1991), p. 32.

7. Mitchell, *The Enlightened Mind,* p. 209. The novice was Hui-Hai, who became a Zen master himself. In telling this story, Hui-Hai added, "From that day on, I stopped looking elsewhere. All you have to do is look into your own mind; then the marvelous reality will manifest itself at all times" (p. 56).

8. Mitroff and Denton, *A Spiritual Audit of Corporate America,* pp. xv–xvi. Emphasis added.

9. C. A. Hammerschlag, *The Theft of the Spirit* (New York: Simon & Schuster, 1993), pp. 170–171.

10. E. Kurtz and K. Ketcham, *The Spirituality of Imperfection: Modern Wisdom from Classic Stories* (New York: Bantam, 1992), p. 35.

11. D. Whyte, *The Heart Aroused: Poetry and the Preservation of the Soul in Corporate America* (New York: Doubleday Currency, 1994).

12. Campbell, *A Joseph Campbell Companion,* p. 24.

Interlude: Leaning into Your Fear

Epigraph: Lao-tzu, in S. Mitchell (ed.), *The Enlightened Heart: An Anthology of Sacred Poetry* (New York: HarperCollins, 1989), p. 16.

1. Quoted in L. Dorsey, *Healing Words* (San Francisco: HarperSanFrancisco, 1993), p. 5.

2. E. Klein and J. B. Izzo, *Awakening Corporate Soul: Four Paths to Unleash the Power of People at Work* (Lions Bay, British Columbia: Fairwinds Press, 1999).

3. Cited at http://www.ag.wastholm.net/aphorism/A-1486.

4. Seng-Ts'an, "The Mind of Absolute Trust," in Mitchell, *The Enlightened Heart,* p. 27. Seng-Ts'an (?–606) was a Zen master.

5. Mitchell, *Enlightened Heart,* p. 95.

6. Hammerschlag, *Theft of the Spirit,* p. 50.

7. B. Irwin, quoted in Hammerschlag, *Theft of the Spirit,* p. 45.

8. Hammerschlag, *Theft of the Spirit,* p. 45.

9. Kurtz and Ketcham, *Spirituality of Imperfection,* p. 47.

10. E. Becker, *The Denial of Death* (New York: Free Press, 1975), p. 34.

11. Kurtz and Ketcham, *Spirituality of Imperfection,* p. 56.

12. J. Campbell, *The Power of Myth* (New York: Doubleday, 1988), p. 5.

Interlude: Community and the Cycle of Giving

Epigraph: Rumi, quoted in A. Harvey (ed.), *Speaking Flame: Rumi* (Ithaca, N.Y.: Meeramma, 1989), p. 86.

1. C. Pearson, *Awakening the Heroes Within* (San Francisco: HarperSanFrancisco, 1991), p. 1.

2. K. Gibran, *The Prophet* (New York: Knopf, 1970), pp. 32–33.

3. D. Chatterjee, *Leading Consciously: A Pilgrimage Toward Self-Mastery* (Boston: Butterworth-Heinemann, 1998), p. 150.

4. C. Whitmyer (ed.), *In the Company of Others* (New York: Putnam, 1993), p. 81.

5. T. Moore, *Care of the Soul: A Guide for Cultivating Depth and Sacredness in Everyday Life* (New York: HarperCollins, 1991), p. 77.

6. Guiraut de Borneil, quoted in Campbell, *A Joseph Campbell Companion,* p. 77.

7. Fox, *Reinvention of Work,* p. 5.

8. J. R. Hackman, G. R. Oldham, R. Janson, and K. Purdy, "A New Strategy for Job Enrichment," in L. E. Boone and D. D. Bowen (eds.), *The Great Writings in Management and Organizational Behavior* (New York: Random House, 1987), p. 315.

9. Personal communication.

10. We discuss these and other sources of power in more detail in Chapter Nine of L. G. Bolman and T. E. Deal, *Reframing Organizations: Artistry, Choice, and Leadership* (San Francisco: Jossey-Bass, 1991).

11. M. S. Peck, *The Different Drum: Community Making and Peace* (New York: Simon & Schuster, 1987), p. 71.

12. D. Campbell, "If I'm in Charge, Why Is Everyone Laughing?" paper presented at the Center for Creative Leadership, Greensboro, N.C., 1983.

13. E. Griffin, *The Reflective Executive: A Spirituality of Business and Enterprise* (New York: Crossroad, 1993), p. 159.

14. Hillman, *A Blue Fire,* p. 225.

15. C. P. Estés, *The Gift of Story* (New York: Ballantine, 1993), pp. 28–29.

16. Estés, *Gift of Story,* pp. 28–29.

Interlude: Expressing the Spirit

Epigraphs: A. Einstein, quoted in S. Mitchell (ed.), *The Enlightened Mind: An Anthology of Sacred Prose* (New York: HarperCollins, 1991), p. 191; Rabbi H. Kushner, quoted in P. L. Berman, *Courage of Conviction* (New York: Ballantine, 1985), p. 164.

1. H. Cox, *The Feast of Fools* (Cambridge, Mass.: Harvard University Press, 1969), p. 16.

2. J. Campbell, *Power of Myth,* p. 48.

3. J. James, "African Philosophy, Theory, and Living Thinkers," in J. James and R. Farmer (eds.), *Spirit, Space, and Survival: African American Women in (White) Academe* (New York: Routledge, 1993), p. 31.

4. S. K. Langer, *Philosophy in a New Key* (Cambridge, Mass.: Harvard University Press, 1951), p. xvii.

5. Franz Liszt, quoted in Langer, *Philosophy in a New Key*, p. 236.

6. Cox, *Feast of Fools*, p. 12.

Chapter Fifteen: The Twilight of Leadership

1. Dante Alighieri, *The Divine Comedy: Purgatory*, canto 27, translated by S. T. Massey, in "The Act of Creation and the Process of Learning," keynote address presented at the Cultural Congress, Indianapolis, Ind., Mar. 12, 1994.

Chapter Sixteen: Deep Refuge

1. Rumi, "Why Organize a Universe This Way?" in Moyne and Barks, *Open Secret*, p. 79.

Interlude: The Cycle of the Spirit

Epigraph: A. E. Housman, "Wake: The Silver Dust Returning," in *A Shropshire Lad* (London: Paul, Trench, Treubner, 1896).

1. S. B. Nuland, *How We Die* (New York: Knopf, 1994).

2. Becker, *Denial of Death*, p. 27.

3. Kurtz and Ketcham, *Spirituality of Imperfection*, p. 58.

4. N. Frye, *Myth and Metaphor: Selected Essays, 1974–1988*, ed. R. D. Denham (Charlottesville: University Press of Virginia, 1990), p. 224.

5. P. Coelho, *The Alchemist* (San Francisco: HarperSanFrancisco, 1993), p. 167.

6. Becker, *Denial of Death*, p. 285.

7. A. Greeley, quoted in Berman, *Courage of Conviction,* pp. 114–115.

8. S. Kierkegaard, quoted in Becker, *Denial of Death,* pp. 257–258.

9. Coelho, *Alchemist,* p. 167.

10. G. de Purucker, *Wind of the Spirit* (Pasadena, Calif.: Theosophical University Press, 1984), p. 17.

Postlude: Continuing a Spirited Dialogue

1. S. Trott, *The Holy Man* (New York: Riverhead, 1995).

2. Isaiah 40:31 (King James Version).

3. Matthew 7:7 (Revised Standard Version).

4. R. Housden, *Sacred America: The Emerging Spirit of the People* (New York: Simon & Schuster, 1999), pp. 55–56.

5. Housden, *Sacred America,* p. 58.

6. R. H. Waterman, *What America Does Best: Learning from Companies That Put People First* (New York: Norton, 1994).

7. T. Kidder, *The Soul of a New Machine* (New York: Little, Brown, 1981), p. 287.

8. T. Kidder, *Among Schoolchildren* (Boston: Houghton Mifflin, 1989), pp. 312–313.

9. For more information, contact the Robert K. Greenleaf Center for Servant Leadership, 921 East 86th Street, Suite 200, Indianapolis, IN 46240; telephone: (317) 259-1241.

10. For more information, contact the conference sponsor: The Message Company, 4 Camino Azul, Santa Fe, NM 87505; telephone: (505) 474-0998 or (505) 474-7604.

11. Personal communication, Oct. 1998.

Postlude: Soul at Work

1. D. Stafford, "Energy, Emotion Aid Auto Plant," *Kansas City Star,* Feb. 9, 2000, pp. C-1, C-4.

2. J. Condon, D. Dee, and F. Noyes, personal communications, Sept. 2000.

3. Philip H. Mirvis, personal communication, Aug. 2000.

4. C. M. Farkas and P. De Backer, *Maximum Leadership: The World's Leading CEOs Share Their Five Strategies for Success* (New York: Henry Holt, 1996), p. 87.

5. R. Levering and M. Moskowitz, *The 100 Best Companies to Work for in America* (New York: Plume, 1994), p. 138.

6. Personal communication, Oct. 1998.

7. T. Petzinger, *Hard Landing* (New York: Random House, 1995), p. 284.

8. Levering and Moskowitz, *100 Best Companies,* p. 47.

9. M. Ryan, "They Call Their Boss a Hero," *Parade,* Sept. 8, 1996, pp. 4–5.

10. M. Long, "Contagious Confidence," *San Luis Obispo Tribune*, Jan. 30, 2001, p. C-1.

11. J. Stack, *The Great Game of Business* (New York: Doubleday/Currency, 1994). Visit www.greatgame.com for basic information about this approach and links to additional resources.

12. R. Teerlink and L. Ozley, *More Than a Motorcycle: The Leadership Journey at Harley-Davidson* (Boston: Harvard Business School Press, 2000).

13. Chatterjee, *Leading Consciously,* pp. 140–141.

14. John Jacobson, personal communication, Sept. 2000.

15. Rumi, "Why Organize a Universe This Way?" In Moyne and Barks, *Open Secret,* p. 79.

RECOMMENDED READING

Al-Suhrawardy, A.S.A.A. *The Sayings of Muhammad*. Boston: Tuttle, 1992.

Armstrong, K. *A History of God*. New York: Knopf, 1993.

Autry, J. A. *Love and Profit: The Art of Caring Leadership*. New York: Morrow, 1991.

Berman, P. L. *Courage of Conviction*. New York: Ballantine, 1985.

Berman, P. L. *The Search for Meaning: Americans Talk About What They Believe and Why*. New York: Ballantine, 1990.

Campbell, J. *Hero with a Thousand Faces*. New York: World, 1956.

Campbell, J. *The Power of Myth*. New York: Doubleday, 1988.

Chittick, W. C. *The Sufi Path of Love: The Spiritual Teachings of Rumi*. Albany: State University of New York Press, 1983.

Coelho, P. *The Alchemist*. San Francisco: HarperSanFrancisco, 1993.

Collins, J. C., and Porras, J. I. *Built to Last: Successful Habits of Visionary Companies*. New York: HarperBusiness, 1994.

Cox, H. *The Feast of Fools*. Cambridge, Mass.: Harvard University Press, 1969.

Estés, C. P. *The Gift of Story*. New York: Ballantine, 1993.

Fox, M. *The Reinvention of Work: A New Vision of Livelihood for Our Time*. San Francisco: HarperSanFrancisco, 1994.

Giles, L. (ed.). *Musings of a Chinese Mystic: Selections from the Philosophy of Chuang Tzu*. London: Murray, 1906.

Greenleaf, R. K. "The Leader as Servant." In C. Whitmyer (ed.), *In the Company of Others*. New York: Putnam, 1993.

Griffin, E. *The Reflective Executive: A Spirituality of Business and Enterprise.* New York: Crossroad, 1993.

Hammerschlag, C. A. *The Theft of the Spirit.* New York: Simon & Schuster, 1993.

Harvey, A. (ed). *Speaking Flame: Rumi.* Ithaca, N.Y.: Meeramma, 1989.

Harvey, A. *The Way of Passion: A Celebration of Rumi.* Berkeley, Calif.: Frog, 1994.

Hawley, J. *Reawakening the Spirit in Work: The Power of Dharmic Management.* San Francisco: Berrett-Koehler, 1993.

Heider, J. *The Tao of Leadership: Leadership Strategies for a New Age.* New York: Bantam, 1986.

Hillman, J. *A Blue Fire: Selected Writings,* ed. T. Moore. New York: Harper-Collins, 1991.

Izutsu, T. *Sufism and Taoism: A Comparative Study of Key Philosophical Concepts.* Berkeley: University of California Press, 1983.

James, J. "African Philosophy, Theory, and Living Thinkers." In J. James and R. Farmer (eds.), *Spirit, Space, and Survival: African American Women in (White) Academe.* New York: Routledge, 1993.

Kipnis, A. R. *Knights Without Armor.* New York: Tarcher/Perigree, 1991.

Klein, E., and Izzo, J. B. *Awakening Corporate Soul: Four Paths to Unleash the Power of People at Work.* Lions Bay, British Columbia: Fairwinds Press, 1999.

Kurtz, E., and Ketcham, K. *The Spirituality of Imperfection: Modern Wisdom from Classic Stories.* New York: Bantam, 1992.

Kushner, H. *Who Needs God?* New York: Summit, 1989.

Lane, R. E. *The Loss of Happiness in Market Democracies.* New Haven, Conn.: Yale University Press, 2000.

Langer, S. K. *Philosophy in a New Key.* Cambridge, Mass.: Harvard University Press, 1951.

May, R. *The Cry for Myth.* New York: Dell, 1991.

Mirvis, P. H. "Soul Work in Organizations." *Organization Science,* 1997, *8,* 193–206.

Mitchell, S. (ed.). *The Enlightened Heart: An Anthology of Sacred Poetry.* New York: HarperCollins, 1989.

Mitchell, S. (ed.). *The Enlightened Mind: An Anthology of Sacred Prose.* New York: HarperCollins, 1991.

Mitroff, I. I., and Denton, E. A. *A Spiritual Audit of Corporate America.* San Francisco: Jossey-Bass: 1999.

Moore, T. *Care of the Soul: A Guide for Cultivating Depth and Sacredness in Everyday Life.* New York: HarperCollins, 1991.

Moyne, J., and Barks, C. *Open Secret: Versions of Rumi.* Putney, Vt.: Threshold Books, 1984.

Needleman, J. *Money and the Meaning of Life.* New York: Doubleday, 1991.

Nuland, S. B. *How We Die.* New York: Knopf, 1994.

Pearson, C. *Awakening the Heroes Within.* San Francisco: HarperSanFrancisco, 1991.

Peck, M. S. "The Fallacy of Rugged Individualism." In C. Whitmyer (ed.), *In the Company of Others.* New York: Putnam, 1993.

Purucker, G. de. *Wind of the Spirit.* Pasadena, Calif.: Theosophical University Press, 1984.

Putnam, R. D. "Bowling Alone: America's Declining Social Capital." *Journal of Democracy,* 1995, *6,* 67–78.

Shah, I. *Tales of the Dervishes.* New York: Dutton, 1969.

Starhawk. "Celebration: The Spirit of Community." In C. Whitmyer (ed.), *In the Company of Others.* New York: Putnam, 1993.

Trott, S. *The Holy Man.* New York: Riverhead, 1995.

Watts, A. W. *The Spirit of Zen: A Way of Life, Work, and Art in the Far East.* Boston: Tuttle, 1992.

Whitmyer, C. (ed.). *In the Company of Others.* New York: Putnam, 1993.

Whyte, D. *The Heart Aroused: Poetry and the Preservation of the Soul in Corporate America.* New York: Doubleday/Currency, 1994.

ACKNOWLEDGMENTS

From our first encounter to our production of this revised edition of *Leading with Soul,* our mutual journey has been much more a series of serendipitous twists of fate than a simple, linear path. It began over twenty years ago when the two of us were paired to teach a course at the Harvard Graduate School of Education. It was in fact a mismatch—a Yale-schooled psychologist team teaching with a Stanford-trained sociologist. Intellectual competition and combat prevailed in the early going, but we eventually found ways to combine our diverse perspectives and to create a multileveled perspective on organizations—the four frames that we described in *Reframing Organizations.*

That early exploration into the cognitive side of leadership was deepened over a conversation at lunch with our friends at Jossey-Bass. As we described in "Continuing a Spirited Dialogue," we left that gathering committed to writing a book on the human spirit. It was not a direction either of us had anticipated. Once embarked we found it both more difficult and more rewarding than we had ever imagined. We spent countless hours exploring unfamiliar literary terrain and experimenting with new ways to write. We reached deeply into our individual and shared spiritual lives. Our journey continues to deepen our understanding of life's most important treasures. We hope this revised edition will encourage others to reach out and explore life's mystery and magic, to touch with awe the depths of soul and the peaks of spirit, and to see life as a gift and leadership as a process of giving from one's heart.

In our journey together we have received advice, counsel, ideas, encouragement, and inspiration from, literally, thousands of people. Limits of space and memory prevent us from naming them all, but we're very aware of the magnitude of our debt to the many people who have helped us persist and learn. We couldn't have done it by ourselves.

We want to thank our friends at Jossey-Bass. Lynn Luckow, Bill Hicks, Cedric Crocker, Kathy Vian, Lisa Shannon, Terry Armstrong Welch, and Lasell Whipple all made significant contributions to the first edition. Our new editor, Kathe Sweeney, and her colleague Byron Schneider both provided indispensable assistance on this new edition. The finished book is our progeny, but their assistance in a difficult delivery was invaluable.

We also continue to be grateful to a number of friends and colleagues who helped us with the first edition. They include Pam

Hawkins, Tom Johnson, Linda Corey, Donna Culver, Linda French, Rich Davis, Mark Kriger, Bowen White, Susan Sonnenday Vogel, Lovett Weems, John Weston, Joseph Hough, Cheryl Lison, Gerry Di Nardo, Brad Bates, Teddy Bart, Casey Baylas, Brad Gray, and the late Edward Smith.

We also want to thank the many who have contributed to the development of this second edition. We are grateful to the many readers who wrote to ask questions, share experiences and ideas, and encourage us. Jackie Shrago contributed a wonderful story about her career transformation. Hanna Coen provided several superb English translations of Japanese material. Cliff Baden, Sharon Blevins, Ellen Castro, Jim Clawson, Peter Frost, John Jacobson, Bob Marx, Phil Mirvis, Judy Neal, Lee Robbins, and Peter Vaill are among the many colleagues who share a deep commitment to understanding spirit at work and have helped us in important ways. Lee is grateful to his colleagues at the Bloch School of Business and Public Administration at the University of Missouri-Kansas City, and offers particular thanks to Gary Baker, Dave Bodde, Nancy Day, Bill Eddy, Linda Franta, Art Gilbert, Patti Greene, Dick Heimovics, Bob Herman, Pat Kearney, Deborah Noble, Al Page, David Renz, Joe Singer, Beth Smith, and Marilyn Taylor. He's also grateful for invaluable support from Mary Yung, Rebekah McCauley, and Syldred Higgins. And he continues to appreciate the personal and spiritual sustenance of all the members of the Brookline Group: Dave Brown, Tim Hall, Todd Jick, Bill Kahn, Phil Mirvis, and Barry Oshry.

Terry's move from Vanderbilt to the University of Southern California's Rossier School has added a new cast of colleagues for intellectual support. At the school level, Gib Hentschke and Estela Bensimon have provided excellent leadership. The Rossier deanship has now passed to Karen Gallagher, who promises to continue the tradition of creating an environment where good ideas are nourished. The generous endowment of Barbara and Roger Rossier has helped make all this possible.

At the division level, Larry Picus serves as a wise and supportive chair. Colleagues Stu Gothold, David Marsh, Carl Cohn, Penny Wolstetter, Bob Baker, Nellie Stromquist, William Maxwell, Bill Tierney, and Bob Ferris serve as a solid sounding board for emerging ideas. At USC's Marshall School of Business, Warren Bennis continues to be a wise mentor and valued friend.

Rick Stone of the National Storytelling Foundation and Joan Vydra, an Illinois school principal, have deepened our appreciation for stories and videos. Joe Condon, Dorinda Dee, and Frank Noyes of the Lawndale Elementary School District provided an excellent example of how leading with soul can pay off.

ACKNOWLEDGMENTS

Homa Aminandani continues to keep Terry on the road, in line, and out of trouble. Her continued assistance and friendship are deeply appreciated.

All our children have contributed to our joint and individual spiritual journeys. Janie Deal, now a director of social work in Twin Falls, Idaho, exemplifies in her career the kind of spunk we are writing about. Lee's children—Edward, Shelley, Lori, Scott, Christopher, and Bradley—have all enriched his life and contributed to his learning.

Sandy Deal and Joan Gallos continue to play an integral role in our writing and our lives. As always, Joan and Sandy provided an environment of love and support, leavened with appropriate doses of probing questions and well-deserved criticism, that made it possible and worthwhile for us to keep going.

Our search for traditional sources of spiritual wisdom has brought a new appreciation for all that our parents did to make us and our work possible. Florence and Eldred Bolman and Robert and Dorothy Deal helped us early in our lives to develop an appreciation for the world of spirit. Though it may have taken longer than they hoped for the fruits of their labor to mature, their influence is evident throughout this work.

THE AUTHORS

Lee G. Bolman is an author, teacher, and consultant. His earlier work on organizational leadership awakened his interest in the spiritual underpinnings of life at work. Born in Brooklyn, New York, to Midwestern parents, he has journeyed physically and spiritually between East and West ever since. Along the way, he earned a B.A. degree in history and a Ph.D. degree in organizational behavior at Yale University. He currently holds the Marion Bloch/Missouri Chair in Leadership at the University of Missouri–Kansas City. He has consulted to corporations, public agencies, universities, and public schools all over the world, though he generally prefers staying home with his family or meandering on mountain trails.

Lee lives in Kansas City, Missouri, with his wife, Joan Gallos, and the two youngest of his six children. He is the coauthor with Terence Deal of numerous books, including *Reframing Organizations: Artistry, Choice and Leadership* (1997) and *Escape from Cluelessness: A Guide for the Organizationally Challenged* (2000).

Terrence E. Deal is an author, teacher, and consultant. His fascination with the symbolic side of modern organizations led to the coauthoring of the best-selling *Corporate Cultures* (1983, with A. A. Kennedy). His most recent publications include *Corporate Celebrations* and *The New Corporate Cultures*. His explorations of the world of spirit evolved from his earlier interest in the role symbols play in contemporary organizations. Terry holds a B.A. degree in history from the University of La Verne, an M.A. degree in educational administration from California State University at Los Angeles, and a Ph.D. degree in education and sociology from Stanford University. He is now the Irving R. Melbo Professor of Education at the Rossier School, University of Southern California, and a consultant to business, health care, military, educational, and religious organizations both inside and outside the United States.

He lives amid vineyards and cattle on a hillside in San Luis Obispo, California, with his wife, Sandy, and their cat, Max. He is the coauthor with Lee Bolman of such books as *Reframing Organizations: Artistry, Choice and Leadership* (1997) and *Escape from Cluelessness: A Guide for the Organizationally Challenged* (2000).

WRITE TO THE
AUTHORS

In this book, we have shared a portion of what we have learned
from many teachers. There is still much more to learn. We invite
readers to participate with us in an ongoing dialogue to deepen
all participants' understanding of spirituality in the workplace.

We know that there are many Steves, Marias, and Jills out
there—managers, entrepreneurs, and corporate officers. We
would welcome hearing your questions, your triumphs and
tragedies, and your hopes and doubts about leadership and spirit
at work and in life. If anything in this book touched you, troubled you, or opened new possibilities for you, please write to us.
We are also interested in hearing about the sources and resources
for soul and spirit that are meaningful for you. We'll respond and
do our best to orchestrate an ongoing conversation. Through
shared dialogue, we hope to keep finding new ways to breathe
zest and joy into life and work.

You can contact us in various ways:

1. Through the *Leading with Soul* Web site:
   www.leadingwithsoul.josseybass.com

2. Via E-mail:
   Lee: bolmanl@earthlink.net
   Terry: sucha@mindspring.com

3. By postal mail:
   Lee Bolman and Terry Deal
   c/o Jossey-Bass Management Series
   Jossey-Bass Publishers
   350 Sansome Street
   San Francisco, CA 94104-1310